DATE DUE

BRODART, CO.

Cat. No. 23-221

GETTING STARTED AS A COMMERCIAL MORTGAGE BROKER

GETTING STARTED AS A COMMERCIAL MORTGAGE BROKER

HOW TO GET TO A SIX-FIGURE SALARY IN 12 MONTHS

PETER J. GINERIS

WILEY

John Wiley & Sons, Inc.

Published by John Wiley & Sons, Inc., Hoboken, New Jersey.
Published simultaneously in Canada.

For general information on our other products and services or for technical support, please contact our Customer Care Department within the United States at (800) 762-2974, outside the United States at (317) 572-3993 or fax (317) 572-4002.

Wiley also publishes its books in a variety of electronic formats. Some content that appears in print may not be available in electronic books. For more information about Wiley products, visit our web site at www.wiley.com.

Library of Congress Cataloging-in-Publication Data:

Gineris, Peter J., 1962–
    Getting started as a commercial mortgage broker: how to get to a six-figure salary in 12 months/Peter J. Gineris.
        p. cm.
    Includes index.
    ISBN 978-0-470-24653-5 (cloth)
        1. Mortgage loans—United States.   2. Commercial real estate—United States.   3. Commercial loans—United States.   I. Title.
    HG2040.5.U5G56 2008
    332.7'202373—dc22

                                                                2008018568

Printed in the United States of America.

10 9 8 7 6 5 4 3 2 1

This Book is dedicated to Angelo and Priscilla. They started as my Dad and Mom and are now two of my best friends.

Contents

Contents

PART I

All the Commercial Mortgage Brokers I Know Earn at Least $100,000/Year (Why This Is a Great Business!)

Recently, I was taking a two-hour lunch before going to the title insurance company to pick up a $25,000 commission check from a commercial mortgage deal I had just arranged. I was sitting at my table, slowly enjoying my gourmet meal, and watching the other people furiously gulping down their food so that they could get back to their jobs within their allotted 60 minutes (including driving or walking). I thought about how smart I was, or at least how much smarter I was than all of these other people scurrying around like little ants. Then it dawned on me that I wasn't any smarter than they are. I was just lucky to be a commercial mortgage broker. Lucky and blessed with this talent of putting together two important groups—those who have the money and those who are looking for the money.

I was still thinking about the commercial lending business as I drove off in my new SUV, and later on at the title company, while I lackadaisically leafed through the envelope to verify that there was indeed a check in the amount of $25,000 payable to me. Then it dawned on me. I deserve this money (for one month's work) because commercial mortgage brokering is indeed "rocket science."

Of course I am being sarcastic. The commercial mortgage business has indeed been great to me financially and in other ways, but not because I'm so smart. In fact, I have been in negotiations with lenders while telling myself, "Come on, get it done; it's not rocket science." And it's really not. If you follow the steps in this book, you will see that commercial mortgage brokering is so easy that it almost doesn't seem fair to be paid so much for your work That excitement about this business is what prompted me to pour my heart and soul into writing this book. I want you to make as much money as I make, or more. That $25,000 check was no joke. Commercial mortgage brokering is a great business, and I know it can change your life. It changed mine!

Commercial mortgage brokering is one of the simplest ways to make a six-figure income (and more) without any additional education or training. The opportunity exists—for anyone willing to work hard—anywhere in the United States. The harder and smarter you are willing to work, the more money you can earn. A $1 million annual income is very achievable in this industry.

This is a business where you can guarantee your client a better (lower rate, longer term, etc.) loan than they have now, so prospecting and finding clients is relatively easy. Why wouldn't they work with you and pay you for saving them a lot of money? I have trained a number of mortgage brokers who used to be stockbrokers. As stockbrokers and salespeople, they could tell their existing and potential clients only that they would try to earn them money. But as a mortgage broker, you can guarantee your clients results. A lower interest rate on a loan will instantly save your client money.

During the late 1990s through September 2007, there was more capital available to the real estate market than ever before in history. More people in the United States as an absolute number and as a percentage of the population had achieved home ownership than ever before. The main reason for this accomplishment was the availability of high-leverage financing. Historically, a person who wanted to buy a $200,000 home needed a down payment of at least $20,000 and in many cases $40,000, which resulted in a 90 percent loan or 80 percent loan to value/purchase price, respectively. During the past five to seven years, the capital markets had become much more aggressive in their lending practices. They made loans in excess of 90 percent and sometimes even loans of 100 percent to 103 percent of a home's value. They based these loans mostly on the borrower's credit score, not on the ability to actually repay the loan through monthly payments. Next, when home mortgage lenders had exhausted the ranks of borrowers with high credit scores, they came up with a new strategy to qualify borrowers. They set a very low initial interest rate on the loan, which enabled a very low monthly payment, even at the high level of loan to value. This low initial payment requirement would show that borrowers could cover their monthly home payment with their current income because the monthly payment was calculated with a below-market interest rate. That rate would eventually go to a market rate, and the monthly payment would also rise to a level the new homeowner could never afford.

These factors, coupled with the slowdown of the housing market and the economy in general, have caused a credit crisis or credit crunch. While the commercial mortgage default rate is less than half of 1 percent, all markets have been negatively affected by the downturn in the housing market. Many of the lenders for commercial mortgage-backed securities (CMBS) are also heavily involved in the residential market. CMBS lenders would fund commercial loans based on their ability to package those loans and sell them on Wall Street as a security backed by a commercial mortgage—a commercial mortgage-backed security. Venture capital groups that were buying residential mortgages were also buying these commercial mortgage securities, and they have slowed down dramatically. With no one to buy their securities, many of the well-known CMBS lenders had to pull out of the market and stop making loans. These CMBS lenders were responsible for funding in excess of 50 percent of all commercial mortgages over the last several years, and 44 percent of the 500 billion funded in 2007. Additionally, some banks have slowed down their lending or tightened their underwriting for a number of reasons. First, due to a slowing economy dictated somewhat by higher gas prices, these banks may see their loan deposits decrease—and since banks are regulated by the government, which restricts the percentage of real estate loans they can make as an overall percentage of their assets (deposits), they may have to decrease the amount of real estate lending they are able to do. Second, all institutions are constantly looking to replace loans that are "run off" or being repaid, but with decreasing lenders in the market, they may be seeing less run off and therefore may have less appetite for new lending opportunities.

To you as a new commercial mortgage broker, it may seem like a bad thing that 44 percent of the capital has withdrawn from the marketplace or that some lenders are decreasing their new loan activity. But plenty of new lenders that have been sitting on the sidelines are taking their place. In fact, it is a better time for a competent mortgage broker than in the past, when borrowers could go directly to the CMBS marketplace and get their own loans. But with that funding source slowing down, what you do as a mortgage broker becomes much more important. You are providing a service to your borrowers with your experience and expertise in finding them the best possible loan in a marketplace where they would be hard-pressed to find good loans themselves. Also, no matter who the lender is and what appetite they may have for new loans, they are all always interested in good quality lending opportunities and will still fight for these higher quality or higher credit assets and higher-quality borrowers.

There is no better time than right now to start in this business. As I write, commercial interest rates are low and expected to stay that way for several years. At this time, the residential mortgage business is struggling with more stringent underwriting standards, declines in home values, and fewer capital sources. If you have been involved in residential real estate as an agent or mortgage broker, you should seriously consider at least starting a side business in commercial mortgage brokerage.

WHAT IS COMMERCIAL MORTGAGE BROKERING?

As you drive down any major thoroughfare in your city, you are surrounded by commercial properties such as office buildings, retail centers, apartment complexes, and industrial structures. The vast majority of these properties have mortgages on them. In a nutshell, commercial mortgage brokering is the job of helping commercial property owners find the mortgage that best fits their need for refinancing, building, or buying property.

This book takes you through the entire brokerage business, from underwriting the loan to locating the best lenders to closing the loan to getting paid a brokerage fee. You will learn how and where to find better financing for all the basic product types. Getting into the commercial mortgage business can help you reach your financial goals—additional monthly income, financial independence, or retiring at an early age with money in the bank and no reliance on the Social Security system. The rest of this chapter outlines some benefits I have enjoyed and watched others enjoy in this career.

ALL THE COMMERCIAL MORTGAGE BROKERS I KNOW EARN AT LEAST $100,000/YEAR

Only 3 percent of workers in the United States earn more than $100,000 per year. I don't know any commercial mortgage brokers who don't earn at least that much every year.

When I worked at Domino's Pizza in corporate accounting, I was making $18,000 a year. This was many years ago, but it does give you an idea of a corporate salary. Let's compare it with my first year in production as a commercial lender at Heller Financial in Westwood (Los Angeles), California, just three years after I left Domino's. My income had more than quadrupled to $75,000.

Fast-forward to today. I will produce in excess of $400,000 in fees this year. And I want you to be just as successful as I am.

Here's an example of how the commissions work in commercial mortgage brokering. A smaller retail center—say, a building with a nail salon, pizza store, video rental store, and sandwich shop—will commonly be valued at $1 million to $1.5 million for the real estate. If you broker a loan at 75 percent of the value or $750,000 to $1.125 million, you would be paid a fee of $7,500 to $10,125 for placing that loan (See Figure 1.1). And that is only a small deal, and there is one on every corner. If you consider a two- to four-story office building, that fee would range from $15,000 to $60,000. That means you have to broker only a handful of loans to earn a six-figure income. Or you can work more deals and double, triple, or quadruple that income. The average commercial broker in the United States earns annual fees in the $300,000 range.

There is tremendous potential in this industry. It is literally an untapped resource just waiting for you to learn the business. In 2006, commercial volume topped $300 billion. The fees paid out on those loans topped $2 billion. In 2007, the commercial real estate mortgage volume exceeded $500 billion.

FREEDOM

This is a business in which you can truly call your own shots. Work as much or as little as you like, make your own hours, and make as much money as you want. Another benefit is not being chained to a desk every day. I am usually out taking pictures of properties, meeting with potential clients, and looking for deals. In this business, driving around is actually working.

Figure 1.1   Typical Single-Story Office Property

It is definitely not a nine-to-five job where you have to be in one place for any length of time. You can work from your home, your car, or even on vacation. The downside of this is that you are always working. When I'm supposed to be sightseeing on vacation, I'm often thinking, "I wonder what they are building there" or "boy, that's a deal I wish I'd financed."

PRESTIGE

There is nothing like the prestige that comes from working on the largest deals in your town. Not only are they the most visible but many of the things happening in your area can be fascinating developments. It is extremely rewarding to be in on the ground floor of new developments that 99.9 percent of the town doesn't even know are happening.

It is satisfying to be driving around and seeing properties that you actually helped bring to fruition. It really is a valuable service.

On a daily basis, I am working with the biggest developers in the city. They are typically the people with the most cash and clout. It's a great group to belong to.

WHY DON'T MORE PEOPLE GET INTO COMMERCIAL MORTGAGE BROKERING?

This industry is barely tapped. Right now on Amazon.com, there are 1,852 books on residential lending. Do you know how many there are on commercial lending? Just two. The reason is that people think commercial lending is too difficult for them to be successful. It sounds so big and scary, doesn't it? People think residential lending is much more accessible and easier to understand.

That is true in the sense that most of us have borrowed to purchase our homes so we know how a home mortgage works. But commercial lending is just as accessible, as soon as you understand all the pieces of the puzzle that I lay out for you in this book.

You are going to learn tons of insider information that no one has dared share with you. I am about to let the cat out of the bag.

AN INEFFICIENT BUSINESS MODEL LEADS TO OUR SUCCESS

The reason we can be so successful in this industry is that it is an inefficient business. You can get paid just by introducing your clients to the lender that's best for them. If they could find the lenders themselves, they would not need us. But they can't, so we provide a service that helps people and helps the economy, and we are paid well for that service.

The key to being a good dealmaker in this industry is to have as much knowledge of loan programs and lenders as possible. The knowledge that I am going to share with you in this book is going to put you head and shoulders above most of the competition. However, you still have to do the best job possible for your clients on each and every deal. You are providing a very valuable service and are a big part of a successful commercial development or acquisition.

LIVE WHEREVER YOU WANT

I have done commercial lending in Los Angeles and Albuquerque. I also get to travel to smaller towns in my region to find deals. The beauty of commercial lending is that the fundamentals are the same everywhere in the United States. The larger cities typically have the bigger deals, meaning bigger paychecks, but they also have more competition.

Here are what I see as the benefits of the larger markets:

Exciting

A lot more happening

Change happens faster

Bigger deals

Bigger paychecks

And here are what I see as the benefits of the smaller markets:

Loyalty

Not as much competition typically

Steady business

Reliable income

Better quality of life

For your particular situation, you will have to weigh the pluses and minuses of these trade-offs and decide what best fits your life goals and the goals of your family. But if you ever decide to move, your lenders will follow you to almost any market in the country.

NO SPECIAL EDUCATION

Believe it or not, there is no required education to be a commercial mortgage banker. Even residential mortgage brokers are required to attend classes and pass tests!

So instead of paying thousands of dollars to sit in residential classes for weeks on end, and then pass an exam, you can read this book and be up and running as soon as you finish. It truly is amazing.

NO LICENSE REQUIRED IN MOST STATES

This goes hand in hand with no education required. Because there are no educational requirements for becoming a commercial mortgage broker, there are also no governing bodies or licenses required. What this means is that as soon as you finish reading this book, you are a commercial mortgage broker.

It really is amazing and just another great example of how low the barriers to entry into this business are.

Industries with low barriers to entry (ease in starting up a company) in today's society are very hard to find. Let's review the reasons that there are low barriers to becoming a commercial broker.

Low or no start-up costs

No educational requirements

No licenses required

Work from home

Work from anywhere in the United States

No cap on earnings

Huge annual industry volume

Getting in ahead of the curve

Competition doesn't know everything

Imperfect marketplace — not a free exchange of information

Good luck!

Chapter 2

Selling Commercial Mortgages Can Be a Great Side Business for Any Real Estate Professional

The most successful mortgage brokers are in the business full time and have taken the time to cultivate strong relationships with owners/borrowers and lenders. However, you can make good money on a part-time basis, especially if you work in another sector of the real estate industry. As I write this chapter, the residential real estate market is struggling, but the commercial portion is alive and kicking. Getting into this market can help you through a tough residential downturn. The information in this book will put you light-years ahead of many sophisticated owners, developers, and borrowers.

SIDE BUSINESS FOR REAL ESTATE AGENTS, RESIDENTIAL BROKERS, AND COMMERCIAL REAL ESTATE AGENTS

Let's say you are a real estate agent or lender. You already know the benefits we talked about in Chapter 1 because you are already living the American dream of being an entrepreneur, with benefits like the freedom to plan your own day, the ability to make unlimited income, and the choice to live where you want.

During a typical day, I bet you come into contact with at least one buyer or seller who also owns commercial property. And I bet you never considered the opportunities that come with this knowledge and these contacts. Or maybe you did, but you just didn't know what do about it.

Or let's say you are a commercial real estate broker. You are in an excellent position to refer your clients who are purchasing commercial property to a broker or bank. However, you have to be very careful about how you do this because there are rules governing this relationship. If you are going to be paid a fee, you must disclose it to your purchaser. A future chapter discusses such situations in further detail.

The beauty of already being in the real estate business is that you have so many connections and opportunities just waiting to be mined. You can still keep your day job and yet supplement it quite easily by tapping into the commercial mortgage business.

You may want to partner with a few lenders (as discussed later in the book) and specialize in the type of deals they do. Since you can't possibly know everything about every single type of property on a part-time basis, you will have to pick a niche and choose your lenders accordingly.

However, the best way to get started on a part-time basis is to partner with a commercial mortgage broker. You would be, in effect, what is known as a deal maker. You bring two parties together, step out of the loop, and are paid a very handsome fee for your trouble. Because most commercial brokers do know about all types of properties and the best lenders, you can learn a lot from them. Choose a broker you trust and give that broker all your deals exclusively, once you have negotiated a good referral fee. How to choose your broker is discussed later on in this chapter.

Keep in mind that if you are staying with your day job (whether you are a real estate agent, residential lender, commercial real estate agent, or not even in this industry), it's still important to study the information in this book carefully so you can add value to your deals, even when you're turning them over to a partner-broker.

HOW TO MAKE $3,000 A MONTH IN A SIDE BUSINESS

If you drive down any street in America, you will see $1 million commercial properties on practically every corner.

Let's say you take a $1 million deal to your commercial broker of choice, who has agreed to pay you 30 percent of his or her fees. The fees to the broker on that deal are typically 1 percent or about $10,000. So a few days after closing, you receive a check for $3,000. You could easily do this once a month or just 12 times a year for an extra $36,000 a year in your pocket (before taxes).

Let's say you decide to specialize in office buildings. Every time you pass by an office building, make a mental note to try to place a loan on that piece of property. Jot down the address, and in Chapter 5 I show you how to find and contact the owner. It really is that easy.

By the way, a $1 million deal is the smallest deal I have done this past year. The largest was $30 million (or $300,000 in fees). How would you like to get 30 percent of one of those—$90,000 for just bringing two parties together?

HOW TO FIND THE RIGHT BROKER OR LENDER FOR A PARTNER

The first place to find a commercial broker to partner with is from your Rolodex of friends and business associates. If you don't know any brokers personally, start asking around for recommendations. Once you have some names and phone numbers, set up some face-to-face meetings. When they know you are looking for a commercial broker to refer clients to, they are happy to meet with you.

There is nothing better than meeting in person to get a real feel for someone's character and demeanor. It is also the best way to see how you will work together. Here are some sample questions to get you started.

- Can I get some references from people you have worked with in the past?
- What would a former client say about you?

How much are you doing in annual loans? (A good range would be $20 to $50 million annually.)

- Which lenders are you representing in this area?
- Are you open to paying a fee to me as a part-time broker? Or are you willing to lower your fees to accommodate an additional fee to a part-time broker like me?

If you decide to work with some of the lenders discussed later in this book, ask yourself these questions in choosing these lenders.

- What kind of projects and loans are they looking for?
- Do they have great rates?
- Do they have any special programs that you can promote easily within your community?

HOW TO STRUCTURE A REFERRAL COMMISSION

Once you have identified the broker or lender(s) you want to work with, it's time to structure a deal. One of the first things to discuss is how you will be compensated. Most of these relationships that I have seen are done on a sliding scale.

What this means is that the more business you refer to that broker or lender, the higher your percentage (of the deal's fees) climbs. Brokers and lenders like this type of arrangement because it promotes exclusivity and repeat business.

As an example, the scale may start at 15 percent of the broker's fee for the first deal, increase to 20 percent for the second, 25 percent for the third, and so on—peaking at a max of 50 percent for one calendar year. The sliding scale typically starts all over again at 15 percent at the beginning of the next calendar year.

With your chosen commercial broker, you should get this contract in writing. When you work with a bank or lender, these deals are often done verbally. You should also make it clear that you expect to be paid within days of the deal's closing versus annually. I know of some lenders that only pay out annually, which can be a real bummer if you help find a deal that should pay you $10,000 in January and you don't get paid until the following January. Make sure this point is spelled out in detail.

Now that this very important decision has been taken care of, let's look at ways to refer and find clients. This is the fun part!

HOW TO FIND NEW CLIENTS

Whenever you get a new client, the first question you should ask is "What else do you own?" A more specific approach is to ask, "Do you have any other properties that you would consider financing, whether residential or commercial?"

Let's say that you are a residential lender and have just started working with new clients who are refinancing a $400,000 home, and they mention they need the money to put into their business. Your first question should be "Do you own the building?" If they do, ask if they have considered pulling money out of that property. If they don't own the building, your next question should be "Would you like to own it?"

Now, the beauty of doing this part time is that the commercial broker or lenders that you have partnered with are going to be the ones doing all the work. Isn't that a nice change? They will be responsible for filling out the forms, ordering docs, doing the underwriting, closing the deal, and all the other paperwork and headaches.

MARKETING IDEAS FOR REACHING YOUR CURRENT CLIENTS

As a real estate agent, residential lender, or commercial real estate agent, you should already have a great list of your clients at your fingertips. Here are some good ways to let them know about your commercial loan capability.

Do a Mailing with the USPS: In today's digital delivery society, a postcard or letter in the mail actually stands out. You can announce that you are now a commercial lending broker and would love to help your clients take out money from existing properties at very low rates or help them purchase new investments.

Newsletters by USPS: Many Realtors already mail a monthly newsletter to their clients. Add a special section or paragraph called "The Commercial Corner." In the first issue, announce that you are now a commercial lending broker. In future issues, explain the low commercial lending rates, discuss new commercial developments in your city, or write about related commercial topics.

Monthly or Weekly E-Zine: Write a monthly or weekly e-zine (an e-mail newsletter) that goes out to your client base. Once again, announce your new venture into commercial lending and include an interesting tidbit about commercial property in each issue.

One-Time E-Blast: Instead of writing a weekly or even monthly e-mailed newsletter, do a one-time e-blast to all of your clients to announce your new venture. Tell them that you can't wait to help them with their commercial needs, just as you have helped them with their residential needs.

Have a Party: Hold a reception, a wine and cheese party, or even an elaborate dinner party to announce your new title. Work the room, and let all your clients know about all the new services you are offering.

NETWORKING TO REACH NEW CLIENTS

Networking is where you get the opportunity to add new clients to your database and really get out into the field. There are many places you can do this, and here are a few suggestions.

Farming: Well, in the real estate business it used to be called farming. It is basically just going door to door in a certain neighborhood, handing out business cards, and telling people about the services you offer. So, go door to door in commercial areas doing the same. What have you got to lose? Nothing!

Chamber of Commerce: If you aren't already a member of your local group, join now! Let everyone know about your new venture.

Charity Events: Sign up and attend every charity event in your city. Become well known, and be a patron. Not only will you feel good about donating but you will meet most of your city's movers and shakers.

Alumni Events: Start thinking about alumni events. What high school or college did you attend? Are there any events in your city or in neighboring cities for these institutions? No one is more loyal than a fellow graduate. Start attending these events, even if you have to drive several hours. I guarantee that it will pay off.

Board of Realtors: I am assuming that if you are in residential lending or sales, you already belong. Use these meetings as an opportunity to pass out your new business card as a commercial broker.

Talk to Business Owners: In my city, I frequent many businesses. I am actually quite loyal. I use the same dry cleaners, I order pizza from the same restaurant, and every month I take my dogs to the same place to be groomed. Start talking to the owners of these businesses, and hand out your business card.

Title and Escrow Companies: Every real estate transaction has to go through a title and escrow company. Get in there immediately, and start handing out your new business cards. If you are in the residential business already, they know you and respect you (hopefully). Let them know that you can offer that same level of service for their commercial clients.

DO COMMERCIAL MORTGAGE BROKERS EVER GIVE REFERRALS TO REAL ESTATE AGENTS OR RESIDENTIAL LENDERS?

Something that I am asked all the time is "Since you are a commercial broker, do you ever refer in the opposite direction with residential transactions or commercial purchases?" And my answer is "Yes, I do." However, when I refer (usually to a Realtor or a residential lender), it is quid pro quo. That is, I don't ask for money, but I expect later on to receive a referral from them. If after I make several referrals, nothing is coming back my way, I pick a different party to refer to.

I have several of these very lucrative relationships established, and I value them quite highly. You should cultivate the same types of relationships but only if they don't compete with your current line of business.

BENEFITS

As a fitting end to this chapter, here are some very positive benefits that you will be offering to your existing and new clients. It is very exciting to be involved in a business that can really help people.

Now, let's see how you are helping your clients.

Take Out Money: Many of your clients who own commercial real estate may not even realize that they have untapped equity. You can show them that there is money that can be pulled out to pay off higher-rate loans or to further expand their investment portfolio.

Bring Them the Knowledge That Commercial Rates Are Still Low: Most people are not aware that commercial rates are still at a very low rate, very near their all-time low. Let your clients know about this.

Offer More Services: All of a sudden, you are offering your clients more options. You are a one-stop shop and more diversified. They already enjoy working with you, and now they can work with you on more deals.

Repeat Business: With your new service, you are laying the foundation for more repeat business. Your clients don't have to go to somebody at the local bank for their commercial loan and to you for the residential, and they will probably get a lower commercial rate from you because you are working with a broker who has more options than the bank. Clients know that both types of loans can now be handled by you—someone they know and trust. A great benefit!

Providing Services That Borrowers May Not Know Exist: Your clients may not know that they can take out 80 percent plus 10 percent on a 90 percent occupied building. They may have no clue that this is their solution to paying for their children's college tuition. What a joy to be able to share that information with them.

The bottom line is that part-time commercial mortgage brokering and referrals can be an exciting and lucrative way to supplement your income.

Chapter 3

How to Break into the Business: Getting Training and Getting Started

Everyone has a different approach for starting something new. Some people like to take classes first and get some initial education. Some people like to have some personal training, and some like to just jump in with both feet.

When I started in the lending business, I knew very little about it, and there were no books like this available. I took a class offered by the Mortgage Bankers Association (http://www .mortgagebankers.org/) called Income Property Finance I. It was a good introduction to working with income-producing properties and the financial analysis that goes along with commercial property finance. I find it more valuable for finance than the similar CCIM courses. But as real estate brokers, you may have already taken these classes, and this will aid you in this new discipline of mortgage brokerage as well. For non real brokers or salespersons, a Certified Commercial Investment Member (CCIM) is a recognized expert in the disciplines of commercial and investment real estate. A CCIM is an invaluable resource to the commercial real estate owner, investor, and user, and is among an elite corps of more than 9,000 professionals who hold the CCIM designation across North America and more than 30 countries. Nearly 10,000 additional professionals are pursuing the CCIM designation (taken from the CCIM website http://www .ccim.com/about/ccim.html).

The easiest way to break into the business is to join a firm, start at the bottom as an analyst, and learn the business from experienced professionals already in the brokerage business.

Another approach is to read publications and this book to see what lenders are financing what properties and then go find a deal and start what we call "dialing for dollars."

Another approach is to learn the business from the lender's perspective and then go out on your own or join a firm. In the industry, when a lender switches to the mortgage brokerage side, we refer to that as "joining the dark side." And when someone goes from being a broker to being on the lending side, it is usually to gain more security and a consistent paycheck. Lenders go without commissions but are eligible for a discretionary annual bonus— and bonuses have been very large over the past 10 years. It is very common for individuals to change between the two sides of the business and for lenders to switch institutions fairly often as well. Good people are always in demand in this industry.

HOW TO GET TO THAT SIX-FIGURE INCOME AND BEYOND

I have explained and reviewed the steps in the lending process for you in previous chapters. You should now have a good understanding of how the process works, what lenders are looking for in a loan and a loan submission, and what responsibilities you have in the process.

The next step is to decide how you want to approach your business. The economics are easy. As a mortgage broker, you are paid an origination fee or commission fee of 1 percent of the loan amount you provide. If you want to make $100,000 per year, that is $10 million worth of loans if you are working alone and do not split the fee with another broker or firm. If you are splitting the fees fifty-fifty, then that is $20 million in loan production. The average small retail shop on any main street in the United States or any shadow anchor Wal-Mart retail space is valued at $1.5 to $4 million, and that value equates to $1.1 to $3 million in loan production. Based on this analysis, you may say that I want to work only on larger deals because they pay more fees. That makes sense, except all of your competition also understands that as well, so they are also focusing only on larger deals.

Sometimes it is better to try to fly a little under the radar so you can still make your money and not have the stress of competing on every deal.

Now that you understand the economics, you again need to determine whether you are going to jump in full time or work on mortgages part time and keep your day job. Another approach, as we discussed at the beginning of the book, is to concentrate on referrals. If you are already in the residential real estate business, this is an easy way to supplement your income. You need to find a mortgage broker, such as me, who is willing to accept your referrals and pay you for them. Then you and the mortgage banker need to decide how you will be paid. You may want to be paid a percentage of the fee I am being paid, say, 10 percent to 25 percent, or you may want to be paid a flat fee of, say, $2,000 to $5,000 for each referral.

If you decide to join an existing mortgage banking firm, you are likely to start as an analyst, not as a loan producer. You will probably share, to some extent, in the fees of the broker with whom you are working.

Eventually, you will move into production full time after paying your dues by learning the business from the ground up and working through the topics I discuss in this book. Working with experienced mortgage bankers or brokers is a very beneficial way to learn the business. You can see and work with a variety of styles and also learn basic guidelines the firm has instituted.

If you are a residential mortgage broker, you want to get out of that business as soon as possible. That business will have such scrutiny and regulation over at least the next 12–24 months that completing any deals will be difficult.

The least painful way to start in this business is the referral approach. Find one or more deals, refer them to an experienced mortgage broker, and then try to stay as involved as possible with them as they go through the process. This is a great way to learn and get paid.

It is very possible to push the limits of the six-figure income in this business. I work by the baseball philosophy that you want to hit singles, doubles, triples, and then home runs. You do not want your business and income to be feast or famine; you want to make it as consistent as possible (and hopefully with some high peaks along the way!). Consistency allows you the ability to work smarter, more ethically, and more productively. If you spend your time only working on very large deals you will in inevitably find yourself more stressed, pushing harder with lenders to make loans they do not want to make, and under constant pressure when these deals don't materialize especially if you are working on only commission income—no draws or salaries.

Large deals also tend to lead to spending money before the deal is closed—thinking I am going to earn so much on this deal that I can spend some extra and still have the money I need for ongoing expenses. I like to always have a deal in closing; maybe it is only a one-million-dollar deal, but that is still a $10,000 fee and that, as they say, keeps the lights on. Those loans are usually much easier to find and have less competition because they are not the "sexy" headline deals many brokers like to make. While I have those bases covered, I also like to always have a few medium deals and at least one big deal in the pipeline on some basis. It may be a large power center that is still under construction and not ready for financing right now; I still keep it on my radar and on my potential deal production list. Some broker will probably end up with that deal, but often times it is just the luck of running into the borrower when he is ready to go. You can't depend on those big deals, but you have to keep a few around because a $30-million deal can pay at least a $150,000 fee and possibly a full 1 percent or $300,000 fee. It is a great business, but if you want to be in business for the long run, which you should want, you must have some discipline.

Lesson Learned

I knew a fast-talking broker who fell into a big deal early on in his career. He decided that he was too big for small deals and and never even tried to chase smaller deals or get to know how small deals get done, or who were the borrowers or lenders to focus on for them. And remember, small deals are paying a full 1 percent fee which is 410,000 to $20,000 per deal. He spent all his time on big deals and only big deals. When he couldn't find the next big deal and also those big deals became so competitive that they started paying much less than the typical 1 percent fee, he got to a point that he could no longer pay his bills, ruined his credit rating, and had to quit the business to take a job with a fixed income that was much less than he would have earned if he simply followed this philosophy.

Chapter 4

Overview of a Typical Commercial Mortgage Deal

There are eight basic steps in a typical deal, which I outline here and describe in detail in the next chapters. Those of you who are residential real estate mortgage lenders or real estate brokers will find the steps familiar, but the process is more involved than a residential mortgage deal. Those of you who are already in a commission-based job will find some of the steps similar to what you are now doing.

THE EIGHT BASIC STEPS

A typical deal takes about 60 days from loan application to loan closing and funding, with 30 days for loan approval and then an additional 30 days for documentation and funding. The general steps and order of the commercial mortgage brokerage deal are as follows.

1. The most important and first step in the process is to find a property to finance, that is, either find an owner you can convince to refinance or find a buyer or seller who needs financing to close a real estate sale. You will need to discuss and understand what the borrower is trying to accomplish with the financing and what the long-term goals are for the property.

2. Next, you have to analyze, or underwrite, the loan to see if the economics of the loan request make sense. Underwriting includes inspecting the property and gathering financial information about the property. In many deals, you will know by your first property visit if you can meet the borrower's needs for financing.

3. Next, you complete what I refer to as the preliminary loan submission.

4. Once you are ready to present your deal, find a lender and present the deal.
5. The next step is (hopefully) a loan quote from the lender, which you present to the borrower. This is called issuing a loan quote. In this step, you should receive a loan application from the lender and negotiate any terms as necessary.
6. If the quote is acceptable to the borrower—your client—you move to the loan approval stage, when you will receive the loan commitment.
7. The next step is to get the loan closed and funded. This involves a lot of steps dealing with third parties such as appraisers and title companies.
8. The final step is to collect your commission check and determine what ongoing obligations, if any, you have to the lender on that recently funded loan.

That is the typical process, but in some cases the order of the steps may be changed or you may be working on more than one step simultaneously. For example, you may be working on step 2, analyzing the deal, and also be calling several lenders to see how they would view or price the deal. Sometimes I get a call from a lender looking to finance certain property types, and I then focus on finding those property types for that lender, which means step 4 is completed prior to step 1.

WHAT TYPES OF PROPERTIES CAN I FINANCE?

There is a lender for every type of commercial property in the country. There are lenders that finance many types of commercial properties, and there are some that specialize in certain types.

Commercial real estate property can be loosely defined as all real estate properties that are not residential in nature. You can also add apartment complexes and senior retirement facilities to the category of commercial property; although people live in them, they are run as businesses. Only single-family residences are not considered commercial property. However, even these have an aspect of commercial lending because a developer of single-family homes has to acquire the land and build the infrastructure before selling the lots or building the houses, so this is a commercial acquisition and development loan.

The most common commercial loans, however, are the buildings you see when you drive down any major commercial thoroughfare in the world (See Figure 4.1). You see retail stores, office buildings, apartment complexes, industrial facilities, fast-food stores, restaurants, grocery stores, self-storage units, hotels, medical facilities, and mobile home parks. These are the property types you will be able to finance as quickly as you can locate owners who want financing. These property types are discussed in more detail in Chapter 7, but in the meantime you'll see dollar signs on the side of all commercial properties you drive by (as they do for all of us in the business!).

WHAT IS THE DIFFERENCE BETWEEN A MORTGAGE BROKER AND A MORTGAGE BANKER?

A mortgage broker normally has no special relationship with the lender to whom they bring loan business and borrowers. They simply work on behalf of the borrower to obtain the most attractive real estate financing available in the marketplace, based on the borrower's specific needs or request.

Figure 4.1 Typical Retail Strip Center

Once the loan is approved or closed, the mortgage broker has no more interaction with the borrower or lender regarding that particular transaction.

By contrast, a mortgage banker normally has a much closer relationship with the lender and is responsible for collecting interest payments, completing property inspections, and acting as the intermediary between the borrower and the lender for the life of the loan. The mortgage banker is paid a servicing fee for handling these responsibilities. In most cases, this relationship between the lender and the mortgage banker is called a correspondent relationship; the mortgage banker acts as the correspondent for the lender. This topic is further discussed in Chapter 9 in the context of examining the different types of lenders.

FIDUCIARY RESPONSIBILITIES OF MORTGAGE BROKERS AND MORTGAGE BANKERS

Mortgage brokers' only fiduciary responsibility is to the borrowers they represent. Brokers should be concerned only with the borrower's best interests, and 100 percent of their negotiations should be on the borrower's behalf.

The mortgage banker's fiduciary responsibility is a little more difficult to identify. Mortgage bankers are acting as a correspondent for the lender and yet also representing the borrower. It is the mortgage banker's obligation to bring both the deal and the borrower to the lender, resulting in the banker having a fiduciary responsibility to both parties.

The mortgage banker must be very careful in negotiating on behalf of both parties so as not to behave in a manner that violates this fiduciary relationship. The banker must disclose all information relating to the borrower, property and market even in the event it may cause the lender not to move forward on a transaction. This is a very delicate position to be in and the mortgage banker must be careful not to let the gain or potential loss of a brokerage fee affect their decision making in this area.

Lesson Learned

I knew a mortgage banker, Jeff, a number of years ago who had started a hotel refinance transaction with a borrower and a lender for whom he was a correspondent. The lender had issued a loan application, and while completing his due diligence for his lender loan submission, Jeff discovered that a different and far superior hotel was going to break ground for construction very soon. Jeff knew that the new property would most likely have a negative impact on his borrower's finances by taking business away.

Jeff did not reveal this information to his lender, and after the loan closed and funded, the lender discovered that Jeff had known about the new property. Jeff had not disclosed this information because he thought the lender would not move forward with the loan and he would not get paid his brokerage fee. The lender fired Jeff as the firm's mortgage banker correspondent, and he was never allowed to take loan business to that lender again.

In the case of a mortgage broker, without a lender correspondent relationship, the lender is responsible for completing its own due diligence.

Mortgage brokers and mortgage bankers typically have relationships with multiple lending sources to which they will market a financing package on behalf of the borrower. Experienced mortgage brokers have a vast knowledge of lenders and loan programs and typically tailor their marketing to those lenders that provide loans along the terms the borrower requests. Not all borrowers (and their loan requests) are created equal, nor are all lenders (and their lending programs) created equal, so the most important duty of the mortgage broker is to match the borrower to the appropriate lender.

An experienced mortgage broker listens carefully and asks the correct questions to determine exactly what type of loan and lender the borrower is requesting.

Lesson Learned

I remember how excited I was when I began working with a borrower on a $2.5 million loan early in my career. This loan represented a fee of $25,000 in just 60 short days. I knew the borrowers were also talking to another mortgage broker, and I was determined to find the most loan dollars at the lowest rate available in the market as quickly as possible and beat out my competition. While I talked to my potential first gravy train, my mind was racing, thinking about what lenders I would call about this deal as soon as I walked out of the borrower's office.

I diligently called my lenders, sent out my loan packages, and got back all my loan quotes. I was sure I had the lowest rate available. I knew the lenders I called could beat anyone's rate, and they hadn't even been called or seen the deal from my competition. I quickly sent out my loan quotes to the borrower, reviewed them with him, and gave him a day to evaluate and decide.

The next day when I called my borrower, he informed me that he had already signed a loan application with my competitor. I could not believe my ears! When I asked him by how much my competitor had beaten my interest rate, he said, "Their rate was higher, but that wasn't my biggest hot button on this financing request."

I didn't listen and determine exactly what the borrower was looking for, but I certainly heard that $25,000 broker's fee going into my competitor's bank account!

You must understand that you are not always looking for the lowest interest rate or the highest loan to value; you are looking to provide the most attractive financing that matches the borrower's needs. Many other terms of a loan must be considered, not just rate and loan proceeds.

HOW BROKERS ARE PAID

Both the mortgage banker and the mortgage broker are paid by the borrower. The standard fee is 1 percent of the loan amount. In the case of a $2.5 million loan, the fee would be $25,000.

In addition to this fee, a mortgage banker may also receive a servicing fee, which is normally between 0.03 percent and 0.06 percent per year. For example, on the same $2.5 million loan, the annual servicing fee would be $750 to $1,500 per year.

A third potential fee comes from what is referred to as yield spread premium or a back-end fee, both of which are paid by the lender to the mortgage broker. This type of fee is generally not available in a correspondent mortgage banking relationship but is common in many mortgage broker relationships.

In most cases, this fee is ultimately paid by the borrower in the form of a higher interest rate. This type of fee should always be disclosed to borrowers because its impact is really working against their obtaining the lowest interest rate available. In some instances, the borrower requests a fee to be paid in this manner, which is addressed in Chapter 5.

PART II

Chapter 5

How Do I Find My First Deal?

In the early going, finding a deal can be the most difficult part of the process. (The other hard part is closing and loan document negotiation—when I always wish I was back on the street finding deals.)

Until you have been in the business long enough to build up a clientele of borrowers who will call you with every new deal, you will have to make a concerted effort to find deals. The most efficient deal to find is a deal that is looking for financing. That is, a borrower is already in the market and wants to refinance an existing property or acquire a new property. Of course, not every property is need of financing, and not all owners know they should or need to refinance their higher-rate loan.

The most important thing to remember when considering a deal is to think about whether you should just say no. I have seen plenty of brokers be less productive by saying yes to deals that will consume all their time and possibly never get funded. You never want to get so caught up in one loan request that you pass up or miss many others that could be easily sent to a willing lender. Don't make a career out of one deal.

Also remember that bigger deals pay more, but they usually have more people working on them and are less likely to come to fruition for you. My philosophy is first singles, doubles, and triples and then home runs. All brokers always have some $30 million deal floating around their desks, but they also have lots of $1 million to $5 million loans that keep all the lights on and their mortgages paid. Also keep in mind that the larger the loan, the more likely the borrower is to expect you to cut your fee, and your competitors may very well have already cut theirs to win the business. It is the old philosophy that half a percent of something is better than 1 percent of nothing. On the other hand, the $1 million to $5 million borrowers rarely expect you to cut your fee.

CONSTRUCTION LOAN TAKE-OUTS

The lowest-hanging fruit are the deals that are in the marketplace looking for debt. They are new properties under construction, nearing completion, or in the lease-up phase. They are typically on a construction or interim loan that will need to be replaced, or what we call taken out. The take-out loan (or sometimes just referred to as the take out) is typically a long-term loan with a low fixed rate that will replace or take out the bank construction loan, which is typically at a higher floating rate with a maturity date of less than five years and sometimes just 18 to 24 months. The banks or construction lenders typically would like to keep these loans on their books and often offer the borrower a short-term permanent loan known as a mini-perm. Mini-perms are usually for a term of five years or less and at a bank rate that is usually higher than the rates of the lenders with whom you and I will be dealing.

So keep in mind for these deals that we are competing with the lender that has the construction loan already in place; we can't just stroll into the bank and ask them for the information on the property to provide a better loan to their clients. You need to contact the borrower directly. If you know who the builder or developer is, you can just call them on the phone, tell them you want to talk to them about refinancing their current construction loan, and try to set up a meeting.

LOOK FOR SIGNS AND BUILDING PERMITS

Signs: If I don't know who the developer is, I usually can find out by calling the contractor who is actually building the property or by calling the architect who designed the property. In most markets, both of these put up a sign at the site as advertising for themselves, and you can call them from that. If there is no sign, you can get that information, as well as the owner's name, by following the next step.

Building Permits: City Hall's commercial building permits records (usually printed weekly and stored in binders) are where I find out what is going on in real estate in a city. To build any property, developers must obtain a permit from the city or county in which they are building. Most permits must contain the names of the owner, the licensed general contractor, and the architect who designed the building, as well as information on the property and building being constructed.

In addition to mining for deals, this is the place to find out what is going on or who is coming to your area. For example, Wal-Mart or PF Chang's doesn't just come into the market one day and start building. This process starts months and even years in advance, and many of these big national chains don't lease land or space but actually own their own buildings, so they are the owner on the building permit.

I make it a habit to go down to City Hall at least once a month to review commercial building permits. In some cases, residential and commercial permits are printed together, so the process is a little more tedious. I developed a form that I use to note all the commercial permits I think are worth having for later follow-up and reference. The items I include are:

1. Estimated value of the property (this is almost never accurate, much like tax assessment valuation)
2. Square footage of the property being built
3. If it is new or additional construction to an existing property

4. Name, address, and phone number of the owner
5. Name and number of the general contractor
6. Name and number of the architect

REFERRALS

Another set of deals that are already in the marketplace looking for financing is properties that are for sale or under contract for sale. Again, I always call the real estate brokers who have the property listed. I ask them if they have a buyer and if they will give me the buyer's name, give my name to the buyer, or both. If they do not have a buyer, I offer my help on the financing side so they will be able to get the deal closed once they have a buyer. I tell them to let me know as they get closer to needing financing. Depending on my work load and the size of the potential loan, I sometimes offer to spec my time; that is, even though I don't have a deal, I underwrite the deal, talk to some lenders, and provide them a general loan quote on a speculative basis.

Commercial real estate brokers can be a great source for business because they are aware of many deals under contract and are in a great position to give you the name of buyers looking for financing or get your name to them.

For real estate brokers reading this book and looking to get into the mortgage brokerage business, you need to be careful regarding the ethics involved. At a minimum, if you are receiving any sort of referral fee, it must be disclosed to your client as a real estate broker. However, if you do decide to get into this business, you are in a perfect position with all your contacts to get leads to many deals, which will make you very successful.

DEVELOPERS AND BUILDERS

Keeping a list of active real estate developers in your market is a must. One thing that is sure about this business is that people always call the last person (broker) who called them. I make it a habit to try to stay in front of the major players in my market. Touch base with them often enough to know what they are doing but not too often to bother them too much. You never know how much is too much.

Lessons Learned

I remember one particular deal several years ago when I knew the owner was looking for financing. He had just acquired the property and told me he wanted to lease a few vacant spaces before putting a long-term loan on the property. I called him once a week for about two months. Finally, one day he told me to sit tight and said he would call me when he was ready for financing. I didn't call him for about three weeks, and then when I called him, he said, "Oh, that's right, I am sorry about that; I got a call from your competitor last week, and we were finally ready to go, so I signed their loan application. I am really sorry about that."

Well, so was I, as that was a $6.5 million loan, which would have been a $65,000 fee!

Keep in touch with those who are in the market making deals. Ask them for the business. I always ask what I can be helping them with, and if they say nothing right now, I always ask them what they are working on. I want to be the judge of whether I could be helping with something.

TITLE COMPANIES FOR OWNERSHIPS AND COLD CALLING

The next approach to finding new business is the always-popular cold calling. Seventy percent of all U.S. properties are financed with traditional bank debt, which normally comes with a higher rate and a shorter term than what you hope to provide. So you have an advantage over the bank and something to sell to the borrower. The problem comes when you try to find out who the owner is. This is where title companies can help. They are able to search the county ownership records and give you that information in a clear, concise spreadsheet. They are even able to produce mailing labels in the event you decide to complete a mass mailing.

What I have done in the past is to choose a major thoroughfare between two major cross streets, write down the addresses of all the properties I think can be financed in that area, and give those addresses to the title companies. Once you have that information from the title company, you can go through it and contact owners you recognize. The next step with the remaining names is more difficult. Because you don't normally have their phone numbers and e-mail addresses, the only way to proceed is to send out letters, flyers, or postcards to the remaining names on the list. This has a lower probability of success, but remember that all you need is 10 deals (at an average loan of $1 million) a year to make your $100,000 income.

Another focus of cold calling is to be property specific. If you have financed a certain property type, for example, an apartment complex, you have already spent a fair amount of time on that property type. You have learned any special underwriting that might be appropriate for apartments. You have spoken to a variety of lenders to find the best loan for that property type and on what specifics of the property type each of those lenders focuses. For example, some lenders might look for only Class A apartments, some want smaller properties with fewer than 10 units, and some may want only student or senior apartments. You have spent time taking pictures of competing properties of the apartments you financed. You have completed research on the submarket and growth potential where your property was financed. You may have spent time on the Internet learning about the apartment industry, the large developers and owners, and the emerging trends in the industry.

If you have spent all that time learning and selling that loan to your lenders, it would make sense to focus your cold calling on that property type. You can leverage the time you have already spent on the deal you financed into more deals of the same type. You already know the lenders, the market, and the underwriting. Also, now when you start calling on owners, you can say that you just completed the financing of a similar property along the terms you just closed under. This experience gives you and clients much more confidence when you are asking them to allow you to refinance their properties.

Many states have firms in addition to title companies that specialize in sales and rental comparables, as well as ownership information on properties. One national company in this business is CoStar. They specialize in providing information on real estate in most states.

RESIDENTIAL MORTGAGE BROKERS' APPROACH

Residential mortgage brokers have an advantage in that they are already talking to clients. You certainly have an edge on others in your marketing because you need to be asking your clients if they own commercial property as well and if they would like to finance that also. You can offer to complete an analysis to see how much of a loan and what kind of rate you could give them, or you can start by asking what kind of financing they have in place today. You are also privy to their personal financial information, so you can see if they are candidates for commercial financing.

Finally, you can simply be passing the word along that you are also providing commercial mortgages and give them an idea of where those rates are today. And don't be embarrassed to ask for referrals.

START AND KEEP A DETAILED DATABASE

One of the most important things to remember about the mortgage brokerage business is that deals never die. They may not close or fund on one occasion. You may lose the deal to a competitor, or the borrower-owner may not want to refinance at the time. Regardless of any of these occurrences, the deal will be back. In one month or one year or five years, they all come back for another chance to refinance. This is because most land owners use leverage to own their commercial real estate. It is very rare to come across a borrower who truly wants to pay off a loan in full and not refinance.

For this reason, you must keep a detailed call log and database. Every time you talk to an owner, learn something about a property, or lose a loan to a competitor, write it down in your database. This is something that only the very successful do consistently. Most people take one of the following options: "I'll remember that deal and all the specifics," "I'll remember to call that potential borrower next month," or "That deal is lost and I will never see that deal or borrower again."

Many commercial real estate owners own more than one property, so you must ask them about other potential deals. Don't burn any bridges, and keep them in your follow-up call log or, at the very least, in your database.

A SAMPLE DEAL

On the corner of Main Street and First Avenue, a new multitenant (6) retail shop has been built. All the tenants except two are in occupancy and open for business. You saw the bank sign on the site but did not know who the owner is. There is a leasing sign on the site, so you call the real estate broker, who tells you who the owner is, a known developer in the community. You call him and ask him what his business plan is for the property. He tells you it is a long-term hold and says he is talking to the bank about extending the loan.

You ask if he will give you an opportunity to provide him with some other financing options. To make it even easier, you tell him you don't need any personal financial information to provide him with some initial loan quotes, just some basic information on the property and leases. He agrees to give you a chance at this financing of the property. You have your first deal!

HOW TO SIGN UP A CUSTOMER: BROKERAGE AGREEMENT/ENGAGEMENT LETTER

In a perfect world, I would always have an exclusive brokerage agreement with all my borrowers. I would be the only broker my client was talking to, and I would have access, without competition, to the entire lending community. This rarely happens to new brokers in the business and only sometimes happens to seasoned brokers. The purpose of this document or a similar document is to form a meeting of the minds of what both parties are looking for in the transaction. You have a responsibility to the lender and to the borrower, but your fee is normally paid by the borrower. The standard fee is 1 percent of the loan amount, but you still need to have that in writing with your borrower. Fees can also be paid by the lender in the form of a "yield spread" and that typically indicates that the lender adds an increase spread to the rate which covers this payment. The par interest rate without a payment from the lender might be .0615 percent and the interest rate with the yield spread may be .0625 percent. The present value of that increase in the rate for the term of the loan is your "yield spread" payment at closing. In very competitive lending times, the lender may just pay you a yield spread without increasing the rate just to win the deal. Your agreement should identify the amount of your fee to be paid by the borrower as an absolute amount or a percentage of the loan amount and if you are receiving any additional fees from the lender. These fees could also come from your continued involvement in the "servicing" of the loan after closing. In the case of the latter, it is acceptable to say "you may be paid." because servicing agreements can typically be cancelled by the lender at any time. This ongoing involvement after funding is discussed further in Chapter 12.

I use three different agreements in my business when I am starting on a deal or trying to win a deal. There are no hard-and-fast rules for this, but I use the following three approaches in the order of value to my business:

1. I try to get an exclusive brokerage agreement that gives me the exclusive right to obtain a loan for my client along the terms they desire. This agreement allows me a certain amount of time to meet the request, and the borrower agrees not talk to

any other brokers or lenders during that period. If I procure the requested financing and deliver a loan commitment on those terms, the borrower agrees to pay me a brokerage fee.

2. My next approach is to have an engagement letter allowing me to obtain the requested financing, *and* I am able to register a list of lenders to whom I have the exclusive right to market the financing request.

3. At a minimum, I have the borrower execute an agreement that allows me to seek the requested financing and says that the borrower agrees to pay me an agreed-upon fee if I deliver a loan commitment on the requested terms.

Having this agreement in writing protects you and makes sure there is a meeting of the minds of you as the broker and your client as the potential borrower. As you become more experienced, you will be able to determine when it is imperative to have a written agreement and when it is just a good idea.

Lessons Learned

I was involved in a larger loan several years ago with a client for whom I had brokered many loans. The previous loans were all in the $2 million to $4.5 million range and I was paid a full 15 percent fee for each of them. This particular loan was 13 million and since we had completed deals in the past, I did not prepare an agreement for the borrower to sign regarding my fee. I was under the mistaken impression that, as in the past, I would be paid a 1 percent fee, or $130,000.

The borrower had done larger loans in the past with other brokers and had always limited the fee to $100,000 regardless of the size of the loan. When we arrived at the closing

---

table, I assumed I would be paid $130,000 and he assumed I would be paid $100,000. Needless to say, this is not the time you want to be discussing this and relying on your borrower to "do the right thing" and pay you the full fee—or in the position in which he really believes he is doing the right thing by paying you a $100,000 fee.

In addition, at this point in a closing, without anything in writing, you have no allies who are going to stop this 13-million-dollar transaction for the brokers fee. Most lenders will protect the broker, but with nothing in writing, they have nothing to protect. We ended up splitting the difference which was acceptable, but what if the borrower had the mind-set that he never paid more than a $50,000 fee for any transaction? That would have been a $40,000 haircut for me rather than $15,000 and with no real recourse without having a written agreement. It may look greedy to ask for that up front, but you want to make sure everyone understands and get that negotiation out of the way so you can all know under what agreement you are working, both sides.

Chapter 6

An Overview of Commercial Loan Types

The first thing I always do when I find a new deal is verify what type of financing the borrower would like or need. The way to find this out is to ask your client two things:

1. What is most important to your financing: low interest rate, long fixed-rate term, easy prepayment, higher loan amount (high loan to value), recourse, or what? In some cases, I have had borrowers that simply want the lowest interest rate they can find regardless of other terms. We refer to this as a country club rate, a rate they can brag about to their friends at the country club.

2. What is your client's business plan for the property? This question normally provides much of the answer to the first question. If your borrower's business plan is to hold the property for a long time, then you know that a prepayment penalty is not an issue for the borrower. If the borrower wants to pay off the loan in full as soon as possible, then you know you should be looking for a loan in which the term and amortization are the same or a fully amortizing loan.

BASIC ELEMENTS OF A COMMERCIAL LOAN

The most common commercial loan in today's market is a 10-year term loan with a 25- to 30-year amortization and a 75 percent to 80 percent loan to value, at an interest rate of approximately 6 percent with partial or full recourse and variable or fixed prepayment penalties. What does all that mean? The basic elements of a loan and loan types are as follows:

A. Term—How many years until the loan matures or is due

B. Amortization—The number of years it would take to repay the loan in full at the current payment amount

C. Interest Rate—The rate that is charged or paid for the use of the money

D. Fixed Rate/Floating Rate—The interest rate can be fixed for a specific term or float, based on some index rate such as prime or LIBOR

E. Bridge Loans—Typically a short-term loan used to bridge the gap between a construction loan and a permanent loan or to complete renovations or a rehabilitation prior to a permanent loan; normally the rates and fees charged are higher than a conventional bank or permanent loan

F. Hard-Money Loans—Typically a short-term loan used when time is of the essence, or for a lower-quality asset or borrower or a more specialized property type; much higher rates and fees than a conventional loan or most bridge loans

G. Recourse versus Nonrecourse—The loan can be guaranteed in full, in part, or not at all by the borrower

H. Prepayment Penalty—A fee the lender may charge to allow the borrower to repay the loan prior to maturity; loans with lower interest rates normally have larger prepayment penalties than loans with higher interest rates or more flexible prepayment loans

I. Take-out—A loan used to replace or take out a shorter-term bank loan or construction loan, in some cases a requirement by a shorter-term lender as a part of their financing, sometimes referred to as an exit strategy because it outlines how the lender will get repaid

J. Interest Only—A period of time when the loan is not being amortized or paid down; the monthly payments are exactly equal to the interest accrued during the period, so the loan balance remains unchanged as payments are applied

K. Negative Amortization—A structure in which the rate used to calculate the monthly payment is less than the interest rate at which interest being charged to the loan; the loan balance increases each month as payments are made rather than staying constant or decreasing

L. Assumable—Most commercial loans are transferable or assumable by another party or buyer of the property; the buyer must be approved by the lender and typically pays a 1 percent to 2 percent loan fee

M. Holdback—A common practice when the property is not quite stabilized in regard to income, such as a tenant who has signed a lease but is not yet in occupancy, or some work needs to be done to the property, such as repaving the parking lot; the items are not enough to prevent the financing from moving forward, but the lender feels more comfortable in not funding, or holding back, a portion of the loan proceeds; holdback items can usually be completed in a reasonable amount of time, but the timing of the loan funding did not allow them to be completed prior to closing; the lender funds the entire loan, and the holdback portion is held in an escrow account until the release terms are met (I have had holdbacks for tenants that had free rent, for tenants that were not yet in occupancy, for a vacant space, until a parking lot was resurfaced, or until a reroofing project was completed. The difference between a holdback and an earnout is that in most cases the borrower is paying interest on the holdback, even though they have not received the money.)

N. Earnout—Similar to a holdback, except the event that allows the additional money to be funded is not as likely; the term comes from the borrower having to earn additional loan proceeds by completing some additional construction, leasing, or the like: The loan must be earned out by the borrower. (An example of an earnout I structured this year was on the financing of a 79-room Staybridge Suites. The owner-borrower was planning to add 29 rooms on an adjacent parcel but was anxious to fund and lock up the financing on the first phase immediately. We structured the loan with an initial loan funding of $7 million with an earnout of $2.5 million for a total loan of $9.5 million. In this case, construction had not started on the second phase, so it was not funding that was definitely going to take place, and an earnout was more appropriate. In the case of an earnout, the borrower is not paying interest on the money and has a finite time to complete the required work to receive the money. In this case the interest rate on the earnout is not determined until the earnout is funded. The interest rate will be the rate at which the lender is lending money at the time of the second funding, and the overall interest rate will be blended between the first funding and the second or earnout funding.)

TERM AND AMORTIZATION

Unlike residential mortgage loans, commercial loans rarely have a term and amortization of 30 years. Most commercial loans are for properties that are constantly being traded, sold, purchased, or refinanced and rarely are held without debt or leverage. They are typically income-producing properties, so there should always be income being collected to pay expenses and the debt service.

In contrast, the traditional home loan was created as a way to pay off in full your home so you can one day retire in a home with no monthly mortgage payment. (This old formula was forgotten before the housing crisis of 2007, as housing appreciation was so dramatic that homeowners started thinking of their homes as investments. It was further exacerbated with home equity lines of credit, or HELOCs, which worked against the idea of paying off the 30-year mortgage in full.)

Commercial mortgage terms and amortizations can range from 1 year to 30 years. The typical combination in today's financing market is a 10-year term based on a 25- to 30-year amortization. The younger mortgage brokers in today's marketplace refer to that as a 10/25 or 10/30 loan. The older or, as I like to call them, more seasoned mortgage brokers refer to that as a 25 due in 10 loan or a 30 due in 10 loan. The advantage of a longer amortization is that the monthly payment is lower because the payments are spread over a longer period of time. The following chart assumes the loan balance and interest rates are constant and shows the difference in the monthly payment for a 10-year, 15-year, 20-year, 25-year, and 30-year amortization.

LOAN AMOUNT	INTEREST RATE	AMORTIZATION	MONTHLY PAYMENT
$1,000,000	6%	10 Years	$11,046.81
$1,000,000	6%	15 Years	$8,396.58
$1,000,000	6%	20 Years	$7,128.67
$1,000,000	6%	25 Years	$6,410.96
$1,000,000	6%	30 Years	$5,965.68

As the chart shows, the monthly payment for a 10-year amortization is almost twice that of a 30-year amortization. The obvious advantage is that the monthly payment is less, and therefore, if the property is operating well, more income can be taken home by the owner. The disadvantage is that the balance is decreasing or amortizing very slowly. There are a number of reasons that these longer amortizations have become so popular during the last 10 years:

1. To provide more cash flow to the property owner to take home.
2. To provide more cash flow to pay the monthly mortgage payments, commonly knows as the debt service. This has become an important factor as capitalization rates, or cap rates, have dropped below the interest rate of the financing. The cap rate is the return on an investment a buyer is willing to accept based on the purchase price. Cap rates and debt service are covered in more detail in Chapter 8.
3. In the last 10 years, appreciation of commercial property has been so significant that owners have become less and less concerned with amortizing or paying down their loan balances. In fact, I think many owners would never amortize their loans if that option were more readily available in the marketplace.

INTEREST RATES

Commercial loan interest rates are almost always quoted as a spread over one of the following well-known indexes:

Prime Rate—Commercial banks typically quote their loans as a percentage over prime. Historically, prime was known as the rate banks would charge their best customers. Prime is not a fixed rate but is based as a percentage over the Federal Funds Rate, which is the rate banks charge each other when lending between banks; it is determined by the nation's largest banks. This rate is determined by the Federal Open Market Committee, which meets eight times year to try to dictate American economic policy and the direction of the economy.

U.S. Treasury Yield—Most life insurance companies and CMBS lenders typically quote their loans as spread or percentage over the yield of U.S. Treasury notes and bonds. This is a good indication of the economy. If the demand for bonds is high, the yield is lower, and if the demand for bonds is lower, then the yield has to be higher to attract buyers to the bond market. Bonds are typically a more stable investment and considered more conservative than the stock market.

LIBOR—London Inter Bank Offering Rate. This is the similar to U.S. prime in the London wholesale market between banks. It is not dictated by the government and is mainly used by lenders quoting floating rate loans.

The interest rate is always the item that is most discussed and the first question that is asked. But as you will see by the following chart, when it comes to the actual monthly payment, the interest rate plays a much smaller role than the amortization.

LOAN AMOUNT	INTEREST RATE	AMORTIZATION	MONTHLY PAYMENT
$1,000,000	5.5%	20 Years	$6,874.49
$1,000,000	6%	20 Years	$7,128.67
$1,000,000	6.5%	20 Years	$7,415.56
$1,000,000	7%	20 Years	$7,708.03
$1,000,000	7.5%	20 Years	$8,005.90

FIXED VERSUS FLOATING RATES

Fixed-rate loans have the interest rate fixed for the term of the loan, which can be 1 to 30 years. Floating-rate loans have the interest rate fixed for only a period of time. For instance, if the loan is based on prime, it will adjust only when prime adjusts. If a loan is based on 30-day, 90-day, or 6-month LIBOR, it will adjust to the current rate of the appropriate index every 30 days, 90 days, or 6 months.

Some loans may be fixed but have a rate adjustment at a predetermined time. The loan term could be 20 years with a rate adjustment at the end of year 10, or a 10+10 term. These rate adjustments can be vague as to the reset, such as "the rate the lender is quoting at the time for similar properties and markets."

LOAN FEES

Most commercial banks charge a 1 percent loan fee. Life insurance companies and CMBS lenders typically charge 1 percent if they allow a borrower to go to them direct, without a broker, but will waive that fee if the loan is brought to them through a broker. This is to allow the broker to charge their 1 percent loan fee and also to provide incentive to the brokerage community to bring them more loan business.

I cannot stress enough how important it is for you to understand from your borrowers what they are trying to accomplish and what terms are the most important to them. What are their hot buttons? Some only care about rate, some are focused on flexibility of prepayment, and some may only care about how long a loan you can find them. You need to be focused on what they want and be aware of what else is available. I always ask, "What are your long-terms goals? What are you trying to achieve with the financing?"

DEAL EXAMPLE

For our strip retail center example deal, the borrowers' business plan is to hold the property long term. They would like to finance the property for a 10-year fixed-rate term on a 25-year amortization at the best rate available with partial recourse, and the prepayment is not a concern on account of the long-term hold. They would like the loan amount to be between 70 percent and 75 percent of value.

Chapter 7

The Most Common Types of Properties Needing Commercial Loans

In my opinion, the most exciting part of this business, aside from getting paid well, and the flexible schedule, is the wide variety of properties that can be financed. As I mentioned previously, if you drive down any commercial avenue anywhere in the United States, you will be surrounded by properties for which you can provide financing. If approximately 50 percent of all commercial real estate is financed through commercial banks, then you can be confident that at a minimum you will be able to provide better financing than is currently in place on at least 50 percent of all those properties you are driving past. I am sure you are thinking, "Yes, Peter, but some of those are hotels and mobile home parks and restaurants, not income-producing properties." Well, that's why you can do this anywhere, because there are great lenders for all types of commercial property. Here I have outlined the different property types and the characteristics of each, starting with the most common loans and the easiest loans to place with a lender.

THE FOUR MAJOR FOOD GROUPS: OFFICE, RETAIL, WAREHOUSE/INDUSTRIAL, AND MULTIFAMILY APARTMENTS

Office

Office properties are anything from a single-story office building, to a two- to four-story building known as a garden office building, to a high-rise office building. Office properties can be occupied a single tenant or by a variety of tenants. They can be old, new, in the city, downtown, uptown, or in the suburbs. See Figure 7.1.

Figure 7.1 Typical Low Rise/Suburban Office Building

Retail

Retail loans are for properties that sell retail goods.

1. They include multitenant strip centers such as the deal we are financing in Chapter 5.
2. They can be a single-tenant retail store such as Walgreen's or Target.
3. Anchored centers are larger retail centers with one or more large anchor tenants, in addition to small shop space retail tenants. The theory of these centers is that the anchor draws customers to the center, and then the smaller shops benefit from those customers visiting the center. The most common is the grocery-anchored center where after shopping for groceries, the customer may visit the movie rental store or Domino's to take pizza home to the family.
4. Shadow-anchored retail properties are retail strips or pads that are adjacent to an anchored center. The strategy is that the shops not in the anchored center, but in the adjacent centers, also benefit from the customer foot traffic from the large anchor stores.
5. A power center or big box center is a larger retail center that is primarily larger square footage retailers grouped together. An example might be a Best Buy, Linens N Things, Michaels, Office Max, Toys R US, and Barnes & Noble all situated next to one another.
6. Regional malls are typically indoors and contain many small shops situated between larger retailers such as Macy's, Sears, J. C. Penney, and Nordstrom. There are fewer of these centers being constructed now, and they are being replaced by the next retail type.

Figure 7.2 Typical Unanchored Retail Center

Figure 7.3   Special Purpose Retail/Restaurant Property

83

7. Lifestyle centers are similar to regional malls, but they are all outside, uncovered, and customers park their cars right in front of the particular retail store they want to visit.

Warehouse/Industrial

Warehouses, or what is called office/warehouse and industrial properties, include anything from small warehouse properties with an office in the front and a roll-up door in the back for storage to large distribution facilities, as well as any type of manufacturing properties. Typically, any property would fit into this category if it has at least one large roll-up garage door in the front or rear at ground level, dock high, or within a large well where large trucks back down to become level with the loading area.

These properties are sometimes also referred to as office/warehouse space or flex space because they often have a large amount of office space buildout within the unit. An example would be a 5,000-square-foot unit occupied by a sign company. It may have 2,000 square feet of office space as you enter the building from the front for drafting and designing the signs, 2,000 square feet of manufacturing space for constructing the signs, and a 1,000-square-foot warehouse garage area with a roll-up door for storing the signs and possibly parking the installation vehicle. There may also be a fenced yard in the rear for additional vehicles and storage. See Figure 7.4.

A large distribution facility may contain 200,000 square feet or more, with parking for many large trucks.

Multifamily/Apartments

One of the most sought-after lender properties is the large apartment complex. Any property with more than four to six units can be financed with the long-term, fixed-rate loans described in this

Figure 7.4 Typical Office/Warehouse or Flex Space Property

book. This is a property type for which there are myriad lenders that are strictly interested in this property type. They can specialize in class A apartments, old rundown class D apartments, student housing near a university, low-income housing, or senior housing for tenants over the age of 55. No matter what type of apartment complex, there is a lender that specializes in those loans.

Hotels: A Fifth Food Group

Hotels have become very favorably viewed by many lenders over the past two years, and most signs indicate they will stay in favor for years to come. Most lenders still look for hotels with a national flag, which means an affiliation such as Marriott, Hilton, and Holiday Inn (Intercontinental Hotels). See Figure 7.5.

Hotels are different from the previous properties because they are real estate but they are also ongoing businesses. In an apartment, office, retail property, or warehouse, the owner has tenants that occupy the building and have leases associated with their occupancy. A hotel has to basically re-lease the space every day. Also, in the event of a foreclosure on the other property types, a lender can hang a "now leasing" sign or hire one of hundreds of property managers to run the property. In the case of a hotel, there are few property managers to hire, and only one lender I can think of would be capable of managing a hotel property on which it foreclosed. Lenders like hotels with national affiliations because their reservation systems give them a better chance of succeeding.

Mobile Home Parks and Self-Storage Properties

These special use properties continue to be very attractive to many lenders because of their consistently strong performance and very low vacancies and delinquencies. History has proven that once

Figure 7.5 Typical Flagged Hotel Property

Figure 7.6 Typical Metal Sided Self Storage Property

Figure 7.7   Typical Owner-Occupied/Special Purpose Property

someone rents a storage unit and moves their items into the unit, they never seem to take the items out. They just keep paying the $35 to $75 per month, and when the owner increases the monthly rent by a dollar or two, it is not enough to push out the renters. See Figure 7.6.

Mobile home parks are similar in that small increases in rents are rarely enough to push out residents because of the high cost of the mobile home.

Special Purpose Properties Such as Restaurants, Gas Stations, Convenience Stores, Oil Change Shops, and Owner-Occupied Properties

This category contains all the properties not included in any of the other categories. They can fall under the "business as much as real estate" category like hotels, but they can also be leased to third parties. See Figure 7.7. In addition to the operating business aspect, they are referred to as special purpose because they are typically designed for their current use, and it would be costly to renovate them for a new or different use. We have all seen a convenience store that has been converted to other retail use, but I can't think of another use for a Jiffy Lube facility. So that makes it a special use property. But don't worry because there are lenders for those properties as well.

In conclusion, regardless of the property type, there is a way to obtain financing for your clients on any commercial income-producing property.

Chapter 8

How Do I Underwrite the Loan? (aka, Does It Pencil?)

In nonbank commercial lending, the primary focus of the lender is on the real estate, and the secondary focus is on the borrower. That is, the lender is relying on the ability of the income from the property to cover the monthly mortgage payments or, as we call it in the business, service the debt. This does not hold true for an owner-occupied property, such as a doctors' office in which the tenant, the property owner, and the borrower are the same entity. In this case, the lender has to look closely at the ability of the borrower's business to keep the mortgage current.

INCOME

The income from the property comes from the tenants in the property. The monthly rent they pay is negotiated and documented in the property leases. These lengthy leases are summarized in a document we call a rent roll.

The rent roll should include the tenants' names, the square footage of each space, the monthly and annual rent, the type of lease, and the start and end dates of the lease. Other information could be included, such as any additional income the tenant pays for common area maintenance (CAM), how long the tenant has been occupying space at the building as this could be a second or third lease term, any notes that are significant such as a cancellation clause, and a rollover or lease expiration analysis. A good example is the rent roll I use (Figure 8.1). This is a document that the lender will want to review in the loan package. A question that I hear all the time concerns when you can count income from a tenant. The standard in the industry is that the tenant must be in occupancy *and* paying rent for the income to be recognized by the lender. In some cases, tenants can hold back.

RENT ROLL											
				0					As of:		< Date >
Unit	Tenant	Unit Sq. Ft.	Mo. Rent/ Sq. Ft.	Contract Rent/Mo	Contract Rent/Yr.	% of Income	Tenant Since	Lease Type	Lease Term	Lease Comm	Lease Expire
TOTAL PROPERTY											

Figure 8.1   Typical Rent Roll Form

EXPENSES

Expenses are the costs associated with the day-to-day operation of the property. They break down into 10 areas.

1. Property taxes.
2. Property and liability insurance.
3. Utilities.
4. Repairs and maintenance.
5. Janitorial responsibilities—normally only in full-service office leases.
6. Professional fees and service contracts, such as accounting fees, landscaping, pest control, or anything else that is completed on a consistent monthly basis.
7. Management fees, the amount you pay to yourself or a third-party manager to operate the property, pay all the bills, lease vacant spaces (of course, you will also probably pay leasing commissions here as well), take tenant calls, collect rents, and all other duties associated with the day-to-day management of the property. This line item must be added as an expense regardless of whether it is actually paid. It is always expressed as a percentage of gross income and usually ranges between 2 percent for an NNN lease (meaning the tenant is responsible for generally everything) such as Walgreen's, where no real management is needed and the lease term is 10 to 25 years, and 5 percent for a many-tenant property requiring time spent collecting rents, maintaining the property, and re-leasing vacant tenant spaces and therefore higher compensation for the manager.

8. Reserves is an account used to pay capital improvements that are usually nondaily, nonrecurring, one-time expenses the owner may incur, such as resurfacing the parking lot or buying a new air-conditioning unit. The owners or managers may or may not actually save money in an account for these items, but you typically add this line item and deduct some amount for the underwriting of the loan.

9. Tenant improvements (TIs) and leasing commissions (LCs). A tenant improvement is the construction work the owner or landlord agrees to complete for the tenant as additional incentive for the tenant to execute a lease, and it is part of the formula used in determining the lease amount. These improvements are typically expressed in terms of dollars per square foot; for an example, the landlord may agree to complete $25 per square foot of tenant improvements in the tenant space. Such improvements include, on a new space, office walls, carpet, paint, ceiling type, a bathroom, fixtures, and anything else that will be part of the tenant's final space upon opening for business. In the case of an existing space in which the tenant is renewing a lease or a new tenant is moving into an already built-out or improved space, the tenant improvements are typically lower and include new carpet and paint.

10. Common area maintenance (CAM) is those costs in maintaining or operating the property that are billed back or reimbursed by the tenant to the landlord. These are billed back to the tenants on a pro rata basis, which means that one tenant who occupies 25 percent of the property's space would reimburse 25 percent of the CAM. These reimbursements are dictated by the type of lease the tenant signs.

TYPES OF LEASES

The lease is an integral part of income property finance because the tenant leases determine the income of the property. The major elements of a lease are outlined here.

1. Landlord and tenant: This section outlines who the tenant will be including any dba (doing business as) names and the name of the landlord-owner.

2. Type of lease: There are two major types of leases, gross and net. In the gross lease, the tenant's monthly lease payment includes all costs and expenses associated with the tenant's occupancy of the space. In the net lease, the monthly lease payment does not include all costs and expenses of the tenant's occupancy of the space. These additional costs are billed back to the tenant on a monthly basis. The CAM costs include, on a prorated basis, all costs outside the tenant's door, such as lighting, water, landscaping, management, taxes, liability insurance, security, and professional fees. These CAM costs are normally expressed as a per-square-foot dollar amount, and an estimate of these costs will be identified in the lease. In the net lease, commonly known as an NNN lease, the rent is defined as a gross dollar amount with deductions for each of these expenses, for example, gross amount net of taxes, net of insurance, and net of common utilities. Over time, the NNN lease has generically become defined as excluding all expenses, and those expenses that are incurred in the operations of the property will be billed back as CAM. In an NNN lease, the landlord is still responsible for the building structure, walls, and roof. That leads to a third lease type, a modified gross lease. This combination lease typically has taxes, insurance,

and management paid for by the landlord, and lighting, water, and some professional fees like security billed back to the tenant. These items and who will pay for them must be outlined in the lease; these details are very important in the underwriting of the loan. The best way to handle the expenses and determine what type of lease you are reviewing is in the expense, maintenance, and taxes and insurance sections. It is common practice for office space in a multilevel building to be full-service gross leases, and in these cases, the lease will cover all property-related expenses including janitorial for the tenant. So the tenant pays $24.00 per square foot per year, and no other prorated expenses or costs are billed back to the tenant. Retail leases can be either NNN or modified gross. Finally, in some retail leases, you may find an absolute net lease. An example would be a new Walgreen's store in which the owner builds the building to the specifications of Walgreen's, which is known as a build to suit, and then Walgreen's signs a lease for 20 or 25 years and takes reconcilability for everything—the taxes, insurance, maintenance, roof, structure, parking lot, and all costs associated with the property.

3. Unit number and unit size: This part identifies the unit number and the size in square feet of the unit, which determines the amount of CAM reimbursements the tenant will have to pay. CAM is determined by the tenant's pro rata share of leased space calculated as the tenant's square footage divided by the total square footage:

$$\frac{\text{Tenant space}}{\text{Total space}} = \text{Tenant pro rata share of space (percent)}$$

OR

$$\frac{\text{Tenant lease } 1,000 \text{ SF}}{\text{Total Property } 10,000 \text{ SF}} = 0.10 \text{ or } 10 \text{ percent}$$

4. Term of lease: This part identifies how long the lease will run, if there are any renewal terms available to the tenant, and what the lease amount would be for those renewals. (A cancellation clause in the lease that allows the tenant to vacate prior to lease expiration is more likely to be near the end of the lease than here. You as an underwriter must be sure to read the entire lease, or your deal may die later in closing.)

5. Start and end dates: You typically have three dates in a lease: the day the lease is signed or executed, the day the lease commences, and the day the rental payments commence. It is very common for a lease not to have an end date identified. You determine the end date by taking the commencement date and adding the number of months in the term (see element 4) to find the expiration date. This is an important concept because when you are underwriting a loan, you are relying on the income, and you need to know for how long the income will be in place. Also, you want the lease expirations, or the rollover, to be staggered so you always have some income; you do not want to be financing a loan when all the tenants vacate at once. If this happens, how will the property pay the expenses and service the debt? Additionally, it is much easier to lease one space than two, three, four, or more spaces. Sometimes leases don't show the start date because it depends on when the tenant improvements were completed and the space was turned over. Normally, there should be a letter from the landlord releasing the space to the tenant or a letter from the tenant acknowledging receipt of the space on a certain date, and that date becomes the lease commencement date. The lease may have a free-rent period, but that is normally part of the lease

term. For example, the lease may be for a term of 36 months, including 2 months of free rent. The lease would still expire after 36 months from possession. Some owners may want 36 months of lease income and thus write the lease for 38 months, which includes the free rent. Leases are most commonly written for a period of years, and the most common lease terms are 3 to 5 years and then 10 years. The tenant who completes and pays for significant tenant improvements usually wants a longer lease to spread out the cost or amortize and take advantage of those improvements over a longer period of time. One question that always comes up when reviewing the leases and preparing the rent roll is when a lease is expiring or coming up for renewal. It helps your argument about renewal if tenants have invested a lot of their own money in the space. If they relocate, they have to spend that money again on a new space so they are likely to stay in the existing space. This is typically true as long as the landlord/owner keeps the rent reasonable or the rent for the renewal period is already specified in the lease.

6. Net operating income (NOI): Net income (above the line) is defined as gross rental income plus any other income plus tenant reimbursements minus operating expenses, from the perspective of a real estate broker, owner, or buyer. For underwriting and for presentation to the lending community, we need to add a few line items. In the income section, I always insert a Vacancy line item, which others call credit loss or vacancy loss. The theory is that although the owner may have a 100 percent leased and occupied property, there is always some vacancy in the marketplace. You cannot stay 100 percent leased 100 percent of the time. The vacancy can be as short as between the time when a tenant vacates a space in a building and the time a new tenant is located, takes occupancy, and

is paying rent. Vacancy is expressed as a percentage, and it is the opposite of occupancy rate. Together, they add up to 100 percent. If a property is 90 percent occupied, it is 10 percent vacant. The rule of thumb in the lending industry is to use a vacancy rate that is the greater of 5 percent or the actual market or submarket vacancy in the area where the property is located. For instance, if the market has a 4 percent vacancy rate, I would use 5 percent. If the market has a 10 percent vacancy rate, I would use the 10 percent, which is greater than the minimum of 5 percent for underwriting. The next item added for our underwriting is a market management fee, expressed as a percentage of gross income. It is the fee a third-party management firm would charge to manage the property on behalf of the owner. The reason for mentioning it here is that an owner of a property with only five tenants usually manages the property—collects the rents, deals with the landscaper, and pays the bills. In this case, the owner-borrower would argue that we should not include a management fee expense because he manages the property himself, and that is true. However, lenders always look at the loan on the basis of what would happen if they had to foreclose and own the property. They would not or could not manage it themselves; they would have to pay a third party to manage the property. So to make sure the property will service the loan comfortably in this worst-case scenario, we have to insert this additional fee. In some NNN leases, this fee is passed through to the tenants, as discussed previously, and in those cases it is not as big a concern to the borrower. We also add a minimal amount, typically $0.10 to $0.50 per square foot, as a capital expense reserve to give the lender a little more cushion in the underwriting. The revised definition for net income and the formula you will use in underwriting your loans for the lender is gross rental income plus any other income plus tenant reimbursements minus a vacancy amount minus operating expenses (including a market management fee and reserves) equals net income.

The form I use for underwriting a commercial loan is shown in Figure 8.2. The gross rental income figure pulls on this Excel spreadsheet from the rent roll shown earlier in this chapter. Take a minute to compare the line items in the form with the line items we just discussed.

We have reviewed all the items down the net operating income line with the exception of the other expenses item that I noted as vacancy CAM. For this example, we assume 100 percent of the expenses are passed through. If I use a vacancy factor of 5 percent, then it must follow that 5 percent of the expenses are not passed through to the tenant. Below the net operating income line, I show additional expenses, which are the tenant improvements and leasing commissions discussed earlier in the chapter. They are not considered to be part of the calculation of net operating income because they are incurred only at the rollover or expiration of a tenant lease and are not consistent ongoing expenses. They are considered below-the-line expenses, meaning they are deducted below the NOI line in the form. Once you have determined the NOI, you can determine the potential loan amount in the next section.

7. Capitalization Rates and Value: The value of an income-producing commercial property can be determined by three methods: the income approach, the sales approach, and the cost approach, which are detailed in Chapter 12. The most commonly used approach and the approach I use in my initial loan underwriting and preliminary lender loan submission is the income approach.

STABILIZED PRO FORMA ANALYSIS				
0				
INCOME			$/SF	
GROSS RENTAL INCOME	$	-		
CAM Reimbursements	$	-		
Real Estate Tax Reimbursements	$	-		
Insurance Reimbursements	$	-		
Total Reimbursement Income	$	-		
Other Income	$	-		
Total Gross Income	$	-		
Less Vacancy & Credit Loss	$	-	10.00%	
EFFECTIVE GROSS INCOME	$	-		
EXPENSES				
Management Fees	$	-	4.00%	
Real Estate Taxes	$	-		
Insurance	$	-		
Utilities	$	-		
Repairs and Maintenance	$	-		
Janitorial	$	-		
Administrative	$	-		
Professional Fees	$	-		
Security	$	-		
Trash	$	-		
Reserves	$	-	$ 0.10	
TOTAL OPERATING EXPENSES	$	-		
NET OPERATING INCOME	$	-		
Tenant Improvements	$	-		
Leasing Commissions	$	-		
Total TI's and LC's	$	-		
NET CASH FLOW	$	-		
Annual Debt Service				
NET CASH FLOW AFTER DEBT SERVICE	$	-		
ANALYSIS				
DSCR BEFORE TI'S/LC'S	N/A			
DSCR AFTER TI'S/LC'S	N/A			
Capitalization Rate		8.00%	$/SF	LTV
VALUE W/ NOI CAPPED	$	-	N/A	N/A
VALUE W/ NET CASH FLOW CAPPED	$	-	N/A	N/A

Figure 8.2　Typical Property Pro Forma Analysis Form

8. Debt service coverage/debt coverage ratio and loan to value: In today's aggressive acquisition climate, the loan to value plays a smaller role than the debt service coverage analysis. Loan to value is simply the percentage the loan is of the total value of the property. For instance, most lenders will not lend more than 75 percent of the total value of the property. Debt service coverage or debt coverage ratio (DCR) is the relationship of the net operating income of the property and the annual debt service, or interest payments, calculated as NOI *divided* by annual debt service or annual interest. For instance, if the NOI is the same as the debt service, then the debt service coverage would be 1:1. If the NOI is $120,000 per year and the interest payments are $100,000 per year, then the DCR is 1.2:1 ($120,000/$100,000). This is an important factor in commercial real estate because the lender is relying on the property to pay or service the debt, and the lender wants some cushion in that coverage for circumstances such as a tenant leaving or expenses rising. Most lenders require a DCR of 1.2:1 to 1.25:1. This can also be expressed as 1.2× or 1.25× meaning 1.2 times the debt service or 1.25 times the debt service.

9. Loan to Value: All lenders further restrict or determine the maximum amount they are willing to loan on a property by limiting their loan to a percentage of the overall value of the property. After the S&L crisis in the early 1980s, the government became more involved in how banks lend money and now restrict the loan that banks can lend to 75 percent of the value of the stabilized property. The typical loans made today are in the range of 75 to 80 percent of the value of the property.

Lesson Learned

I was working on a transaction in the early 1990s, and after completing my underwriting, getting the loan application signed, and moving toward an approval and closing, we discovered a glitch. One of the larger commercial leases contained an early termination clause, which, if exercised, would allow the tenant to vacate the premises prior to the end of the lease, and the property would then not be capable of servicing the debt that was contemplated.

The loan never went any further. Had I read the leases initially, we would not have spent five weeks getting to that point without earning any fee for our time. To add insult to injury, the borrower told me he knew about that early termination clause but didn't think it was important enough to disclose to the lender.

You or your analyst must read all of the subject properties' leases. And by the way, the lease termination clauses and other bad news items are usually written at the end of the lease, just about the time you tell yourself you haven't seen anything odd yet so this lease must fine. Read the entire lease!

Chapter 9

The Four Main Lenders, and What They Want

How do I find a lender and what are the types of lenders? One thing to remember is that all lenders are not created equally. They have different sources of money, and they have different focuses on how and where they want to invest that money. For our purposes here, when I use the term *invest*, I am referring to lending their money.

There are many types of lenders in the real estate marketplace today, and to understand them, you must first know the answers to two questions: First, where does their money come from? Second, what are their motivations and goals in terms of return on their investment or loan? Anytime you are approached by a new lender looking to make loans, you should ask yourself (and the lender) those two questions so you can put that lender in the appropriate place in your lender database.

While there are a myriad of money sources today, there are just four main categories of lenders on real estate property that you will work with in your day-to-day process: banks, life insurance companies, CMBS lenders, and hard-money lenders. A fifth type includes Fannie Mae and Freddie Mac, known as agency lenders. Let's look at each type, where they get their money, their motivations and goals, and what kind of loan production they may complete on an annual basis.

BANKS

Banks are the most common lending institution in the United States today. They are probably responsible for 65 to 70 percent of all term real estate loans in the United States and an even greater percentage, maybe 90 percent, of all U.S. construction loans. Banks are regulated by the U.S. government (FIERRA) and have restrictions on their lending parameters. These restrictions came into light in the 1980s, when savings and loan institutions were making loans that were large in proportion to the value of the property they were using as collateral for the loan—the loan-to-value ratio that was discussed in Chapters 6 and 8. These lending practices led to federal government intervention and, as part of that, resulted in a regulation stating that federal banks could not lend more than 75 percent of the *stabilized* value of a commercial real estate project.

Now, let's ask our two questions: Where do they get their money? What is their motivation or goal in making commercial real estate loans?

Banks are also known as depository institutions, meaning customers keep cash or deposits in banks, and these deposits are federally insured by the FDIC up to certain levels. To entice individual customers to deposit money in a certain bank, the bank pays the customer interest or a return on their deposit. For instance, a bank may advertise a two-year certificate of deposit (CD) interest rate of 4 percent that they will pay you if you maintain a certain deposit amount, maybe $10,000 for 24 months. The bank then takes that money and lends it out at the higher rate of interest that they will get paid, say, 7 percent on a commercial real estate loan. In this example, they are paying one customer a 4 percent rate of interest to get their money and then lending that same money back out to another customer at a 7 percent rate of interest, so the bank is receiving a positive return of 3 percent, plus any loan fees they may have charged the commercial real estate customer.

In this example, you might ask what would happen if the customer with the deposit (CD) came in to the bank and asked to withdraw their deposit. Well, banks assume that not all depositors will ever come in at the same time to withdraw all their money. In addition, the FDIC has restrictions on the percentage of deposits the bank can lend back out on commercial real estate.

Based on this information, it would be prudent for a bank not to lend short-term assets (deposits) against long-term liabilities (loans), so banks are typically shorter-term lenders with loan terms from one to five years. This would also correlate to a shorter amortization period (as discussed in Chapter 6) because the bank is motivated to have its loan repaid as quickly as possible. Finally, with regard to return on the loan or the interest they will charge, it should be in the middle of the pack, not too high and not too little, as it must exceed what they have to pay their depositors to entice them to deposit the money in the bank in the first place.

To recap the bank, they are basically borrowing money by enticing customers to deposit money in the bank to receive an interest return and then lending that money back out to other customers at a premium over what they are paying their depository customers. Banks have other means of obtaining money—by borrowing from other banks, the government, or the Federal Home Loan Bank Board—but these options are similar to borrowing on margin and are typically not used in the majority of commercial real estate lending by banks.

LIFE INSURANCE COMPANIES

Life insurance companies are much less regulated than banks and typically have a much longer view of investment returns. Traditionally, these commercial real estate loans have been much more difficult to obtain than loans from banks and were focused only on select real estate investments.

Let's start with where they get the money to lend. Life insurance companies are similar to banks in that they are also using their customers' money to make commercial real estate investments or loans. A typical life insurance policy has the customer paying monthly premiums for many years until their death, when the life insurance company begins paying the customer's beneficiary monthly payments representing the money paid by the customer plus some amount of interest. Life insurance companies are very sophisticated in analyzing when the benefits will start being paid on any specific customer by using statistics and actuarial tables. They have determined that at any given time, they have a large deposit of cash that may not be used for many years by a specific customer. For many years, they have invested this money in secure, AAA corporate bonds, which do not provide an astronomical return but are safe, consistent investments that should assure the security of the initial investment, as well as a return that should offset future beneficiary payments for customers.

In addition to these corporate bonds, life insurance companies have always invested a small amount of money in commercial real estate mortgages, which were considered riskier than bonds but showed a better return. Life insurance companies were even more cautious of real estate investing through commercial mortgages during the savings and loan debacle and resulting government Resolution Trust Company (RTC) bailout in the 1980s. In the 1990s, life insurance companies ran into their own issues, as many of their corporate bond investments became worthless because of corporate scandal, inappropriate accounting practices, and fraud. This is when the life insurance companies really started to embrace commercial real estate investments. They realized that when a company's stock became worthless, they were left with only a piece of paper, a stock certificate, but if a real estate investment didn't work out, they at least could own a piece of real property that they could sell, hold, or work out. This is the time when many more life insurance companies started lending on commercial real estate, and their lending became much more sophisticated in underwriting and the loan programs that were offered.

Based on this, life insurance companies could evaluate, going by actuarial tables, when payments would need to be initiated and therefore when loans would need to be repaid. This allows them to make loans of various terms from 2 to 30 years and with almost no limit to loan amount. With regard to return or interest rate, life insurance companies were typically used to the lower returns of secure corporate bonds, so a slightly increased return because of the uncertainty of real estate would be required. Their focus initially would be limited to Class A properties and could provide the most attractive commercial real estate loan interest rates.

COMMERCIAL MORTGAGE-BACKED SECURITY LENDERS

Commercial mortgage-backed securities (CMBS) or conduit lenders were begun in the early to middle 1990s, came on strong in the late 1990s, and took the world by storm in the middle 2000s. The Wall Street–based investment banking firms got involved in commercial real estate in earnest in the early 1990s. They came up with a product in which they would bundle a group of real estate mortgages and sell them as a security backed by the mortgages. A security is anything sold on the Wall Street market, a stock is a security backed by ownership in the company, and this security was backed by the commercial real estate mortgage, which provided for interest payments on the mortgage. Those interest payments represent the return on the security or the investment.

Unlike banks or life insurance companies, the CMBS lenders were, for the most part, not lending out their own money. They make loans based on what the eventual buyer of the security (CMBS) will pay for the security, which is based on what return they require, which in turn determines the interest rate of the commercial mortgage.

For example, let's say the buyers of these securities (CMBS) require a return of 5.5 percent to entice them to buy. The lender makes a bunch of loans at a 5.5 percent interest rate and then bundles them together and sells them as one security. The buyer buys them, and the deal is done. The lender doesn't actually have the money to make these loans; it is only making them on the promise that the buyer will buy the mortgage-backed security and just use warehouse or credit lines to make the initial loans on a short-term basis until they are bundled and sold to the buyer. They are a conduit from the individual commercial real estate mortgages to the eventual buyers of the bundled mortgages as a security. This is where the term *conduit* came from; these are not really lenders, but only conduits to the end buyer of the mortgages. This end buyer is really the lender because their funds are eventually used to finance the loans.

As more and more of these bundles of loan securities secured or backed by real estate mortgages have come to market, the more the buyers have started to analyze the individual properties that are contained within each of these bundles or CMBS offerings. The buyers and sellers started selling and buying the CMBS offerings in tranches, with the riskiest portion of the offering receiving the highest return or interest rate and the lowest risk receiving the lowest return. This led to what is known as A piece buyers, B piece buyers, and C piece buyers. Each of these levels or tranches has its own risk-reward profile.

The goal and motivation of these CMBS lenders is not to have the highest rate of return but to produce a large number of loans with a consistent level of return and package them like a consistent commodity. For this reason, the CMBS loans typically have a 10-year term and a 30-year amortization. They are not interested in rapid repayment or rapid paydown of the loan principal; they are focused on longer-term, consistent income, payment of interest. The 30-year amortization allows more available cash flow from the property to service the debt and pay the interest, which is all these CMBS buyers are interested in receiving on a consistent basis.

It is the evolution of the CMBS that has led the United States to what is perceived as a credit crunch: first spreads, then tranching, then no spreads by house (but small percentages of really big numbers), and then subprime to make up for higher yields. The issue is not the risk; it is the reward—where else can you invest the money for the same return?—and the loans were made at too low of a return for some at the time.

HARD-MONEY LENDERS

Hard money lenders are lenders that typically provide bridge loans, redevelopment loans, turnaround loans, mezzanine loans, and quick close loans. They typically obtain their funds from high-net-worth individuals, either on an individual lending basis or as a pool of individuals. They are looking for high returns on their investments in a short period, 12- to 24-month terms for return on more perceived risk than actual real estate risk.

CORRESPONDENT VERSUS OPEN LENDERS

In the early days, when life insurance companies started making loans, they did not want to look at every opportunity available; they wanted to focus on certain types of loan investments. They also did not want to form an entire new division to service these loans, collect interest payments, perform inspections, or deal directly with borrowers. So rather than form a new department to handle all of this, they enlisted the help of mortgage brokers, known as mortgage bankers. They would be the contact or the correspondent for the life insurance company. The lender would not take any loans directly from borrowers or other sources. If you want a loan from this lender, you have to go through the correspondent mortgage banker. There are many life insurance companies that still have correspondent relationships. As long as they are seeing enough quality business, they have no need to change. An open lender would be a lender that solicits loans from mortgage bankers and brokers but will accept these loans from any brokers and they normally do not pay any type of servicing or have any written agreements between the brokers and lenders.

Chapter 10

How Do I Present or Submit to Lenders? (aka, Writing a Loan Summary and a Preliminary Package): What You Leave Out Could Kill Your Deal

Once you have determined the types of lenders you would like to submit the loan to, you have to make contact with the lenders and provide them information on the specific transaction you want to finance.

One thing you must keep in mind is that most of these lenders see many, many loan requests from all over the country. Luckily, as the industry has grown, many lenders have multiple offices with each handling a specific geographic area of the country, so chances are they are somewhat familiar with your market. When I worked at Heller Financial in Los Angeles, I covered 11 western states, and it was easy to gravitate toward the deals where you already had done business or knew the markets—the path of least resistance.

A good loan submission and a strong initial (selling) phone call to the lender can get them on board and behind your deal quickly.

The most important thing to remember when presenting your deal to the lending community is that you must disclose all information about the property up front, both positive and negative. Most people focus on the positive and leave out any negative information. They do this to get the lender excited and hear them say, "Yes, I want that deal. Send me the package right away so I can get started tonight!" But that is not the most important thing for you as a broker to hear, especially if you have not told them everything about the deal. You want to focus on the positive but include any negative information that might affect the lender's interest. Remember, you want to get a yes and an approval to send the package on to the lender because they are interested, but your ultimate goal is to actually close and fund the loan and get paid. Many lenders will be upset if you do not initially tell them all the pertinent facts about the deal.

An example may be a very well-located property, what we refer to as a Main and Main location, going back to the old adage of location, location, location. And let's say that the property is a single-tenant retail store, a sporting goods store, and the lease term, which was originally 10 years, has only 1 year remaining. If the lender is planning to make a 10-year loan and there is only 1 year remaining on the lease term, this could pose a problem for the lender, and it will certainly make a difference in how excited they are on the initial call and how unhappy they will be later, when they find out this fact. I have even seen lenders turn down loans that might otherwise have been done, only because they felt misled in the initial discussion or on the initial call. The way to handle this is to tell them the positives, the great location; the potential issues, the short-term lease; and then why that potential issue is not really an issue at all: In this location, the borrower could always find a replacement tenant.

In the 1980s, after the savings and loan debacle, many of the existing lenders required the loan submission, or write-up, to have a section of potential risks, followed by a section of mitigating factors for each of the risks.

Often the potential issue will not kill the deal. It may just mean that the loan pricing is not as attractive or that some additional structure may be required, such as a holdback, letter of credit, or additional collateral, until the property gets past the one-year lease issue and the space is either renewed or re-leased.

Aside from upsetting the lender, consider it from the borrower's side. The borrower is anxiously awaiting your feedback and, more important, the lender's feedback on the loan request. So you don't give the full story, assuming the lender will figure it out when they get the package, but the lender on the call tells you they love the deal and would price it at 5.5 percent for a 10-year loan so they can win the business. You tell them you'll send the package. In the meantime, your borrower is calling you daily or maybe hourly, including right after you speak to this one particular lender. Because the quote is fresh in your mind and you want to please your client, you pass along the quote, which is a very soft quote even if you had given the lender all the facts. So the borrower is extremely happy and ready to move forward to the next stage. Imagine your dismay and the borrower's anger at you and the lender when the lender realizes your little omission and calls you back to tell you they still want the loan but with an interest rate of 6.5 percent as additional incentive for them to take this lease risk.

This situation causes a lot of stress between all parties in the transaction. Additionally, if you had taken the approach I suggested, the lender may have quoted a 6 percent rate because you had the opportunity to give them the mitigating factors up front. Also, in many instances you are competing with many other brokers simultaneously on the same loan request. Quoting a loan that you ultimately cannot deliver causes you to be perceived as not completely trustworthy or not quite competent, either of which will cause you to lose the deal and perhaps other deals in the future.

> For example, I recently won a $10 million loan when I quoted a loan I knew I could deliver from a reliable source. I thought everything was going great, and then one morning I received a call from the borrower, who said they met with another group that said they could deliver a better loan. He thanked me and said he would call me on the next deal. Many brokers scream and yell at that point, but I told him to call back if things didn't go as planned. He called me back two days later and said that the other broker did not know what he was talking about. He told me he would never do business with them again and thanked me for leaving the door open, and we went on to make the loan.

In the 1990s, when the CMBS market just got started, many borrowers felt that lenders were doing a bait and switch on purpose to win business. Lenders would quote one thing, get the borrower to put up a deposit, and then change the deal according to the credit underwriting department. One company was blamed for this more often than others, and the practice became known as being GE'd. This is another reason you need to be familiar with your lender before telling too much to your client.

Let's continue using the office building refinance loan discussed earlier as an example for contacting the lender and delivering them a loan package.

CALL THE LENDER FIRST AND DISCUSS THE DEAL

It is always a good practice to call the lender before sending out a preliminary loan submission package.

I once worked with a life insurance company that refused to accept any deals without a call first. Regardless of how strong the loan request and property might be, they would set it aside until they were called. I have also sent loan packages only to learn that the lenders were not making any more loans until the following year because they were out of money or had reached their allocation for real estate finance for the current year.

The initial call does not have to be too long and should be focused on the property strengths and any information that *could* be an issue for the lender. The initial quote or feedback is based on the facts you give them, and anything that is not perfect will not kill the deal but may determine how aggressively they quote the loan in terms of interest rate and other factors. They will find out everything eventually, so it is always best to deal with the positives and negatives right up front. I never like to say,

"This is the issue" because then it *is* the issue, but I do point it out.

For example, in our office building refinance, we have several tenants with leases expiring during the first loan year. If those tenants leave and are not replaced, then how will the property service or pay the debt service (interest and amortization payments)? You would say something about the property, something about the location, and then something like "The leasing is good, but we have several tenants rolling in the first year. However, the market vacancy is low, and if they don't renew, the borrower should be able to re-lease the space very quickly." Or review whatever mitigating factors you have for the one concern. Don't emphasize them too much or too little; they just need to be identified. You will inevitably someday have a loan that everyone has turned down because of some issue, and in those cases you just say right up front: "It is a great deal, but there is environmental contamination at the adjacent site, which makes this a tough deal for some lenders." And then list any and all mitigating factors.

WHAT TO SEND IN A PRELIMINARY LOAN SUBMISSION

The initial loan submission, or what I call the preliminary loan submission, should include the following information: a brief synopsis of the loan request, including a description of the property and the borrower; the underwriting you completed; photos of the property, including interior photographs, aerial photograph, and a few street scenes and adjacent property shots so they get a feel for the neighborhood; a map; the current rent roll; and historical operating statements.

Additional information that should help your request includes demographic information and market information pertaining to vacancy and occupancy rates, market condition, and the like. For residential mortgage brokers, information such as demographics will be easy to obtain and should be included. Real estate brokers are used to preparing similar packages and should be able to add market information and other material to strengthen the request.

I typically send my preliminary loan submission in a portable document format (PDF), and I send my final loan submission in a two-hole clasp binder. Many brokers send their submissions in a three-ring binder, which is also acceptable.

The package is typically put together in a loose-leaf or similar three-hole-punched book with a table of contents at the front and corresponding sections following. It should be complete but not a work of art, as this is a numbers game.

1. Cover page
2. Loan summary and loan request
3. Borrower information (paragraph or resume)
4. Market information
5. Aerials, property and area photographs, map, and site plan
6. Stabilized pro forma
7. Historical operations
8. Rent roll
9. Other pertinent information

WHAT TO SEND IN A FINAL LOAN SUBMISSION

While we are on the subject of packages, let me explain what additional items are included in a final loan submission. A final loan submission is what the lender uses for their loan committee and final loan approval, so there is much more in-depth information required in this submission. Most lenders (primarily life insurance companies) have a list of items they need for a final loan approval, which are usually required within 10 days of an executed loan application. Get started on this list fast, because it always takes me longer than I anticipated.

1. Cover page
2. Loan summary and loan recommendation
3. Borrower information: tax returns, personal financial statements, and the like
4. Borrower information: borrowing entity documents (articles, bylaws, operating agreement, and so forth)
5. Credit reports (depends on the lender)
6. Stabilized pro forma
7. Historical operations
8. Rent roll
9. Other pertinent information

HARD COPY VERSUS ELECTRONIC E-MAIL

For the preliminary loan submission, this choice depends on the lender. You need to check with them. For the final loan submission, always send hard copies. If you prepare and print the pictures, aerials, maps, and so on for the lender in the final submission, you can be more confident that the loan committee and credit officers reviewing the loan for approval will see a quality presentation. I don't want the loan approval and my fee relying on how well the loan officer prints out the electronic e-mail package and whether their color printer is working that day. I always send high quality, hard copy submissions to use for the final loan approval.

Chapter 11

How Lenders Decide on Pricing for Your Loan and How to Get the Best Pricing for Your Customer

HOW ARE LENDERS SET UP TO ACCEPT AND QUOTE DEALS AND APPROVE LOANS?

Lenders typically have loan officers or investment officers that are responsible for sourcing new loan business. These investment officers typically work with loan analysts who underwrite loans and complete loan analysis. The underwriting by the investment officers and analysts usually is reviewed by a credit officer to determine the likelihood of approval. Most lenders have some sort of a loan committee of three to six people for final approval. In some cases, the committee members who vote to approve or disapprove are the head of the real estate department, the second in charge, and the credit officer. Sometimes the credit officer does not have a vote but only recommends or doesn't recommend a transaction. In some cases, they recommend the deal, but with certain modifications. Modifications may include additional security, lowering the loan amount, increasing the interest rate, shortening the term, increasing the amount of the loan that is guaranteed by the borrower, or structuring a holdback or earnout once the issue at hand is mitigated. Sometimes loan committees include the investment officers of regions other than where the property is located.

In the case of the CMBS conduit lenders, the real approval lies in the credit officer or member of the real estate group that is responsible for packaging the loans for securitization. This credit person is normally in direct contact with the A piece and B piece buyers of CMBS securitizations. In the event the buyers are not interested in the property for some reason, it will be turned down or require higher pricing—a higher interest rate—to attract the buyers.

Typically, lenders determine the interest rate they will charge based on the risk or perceived risk in the financing. In addition, they consider what other investment vehicles they could invest their money in and what return or interest payments they would receive on those investments. For instance, if they could get a 4 percent return on treasury bills, which have very high quality and low risk, they would want a better return on a real estate investment that has much more risk than a treasury or AAA corporate bond. That said, when Enron, which was considered an AAA investment, failed, many lenders started to allocate more money to real estate because, in the worst case, at least they can foreclose and own the real estate. In the event a corporate bond fails, they have worthless pieces of paper.

The deals with the least risk or, as it's sometimes referred to, the least hair, gets the best pricing.

HOW LENDERS DECIDE ON PRICING FOR YOUR LOAN AND HOW TO GET THE BEST PRICING FOR YOUR CUSTOMER

Items with an impact on pricing are as follows:

1. Market—Primary, secondary, and tertiary markets. Real estate projects in primary (larger MSA) markets typically have the best pricing. The main reason is that in larger markets, there are more tenants to replace tenants that may vacate the property at the end of their lease term. There are also more consumers to keep the tenants in business. Also, their economies tend to be more stable because the loss of any one employer will not have a devastating impact on the entire local economy and on the real estate project the lender is lending against or using as collateral. These three points are available but not as consistent in secondary markets and are almost

nonexistent in smaller, tertiary markets. The overriding factor is in the case of the overbuilding of a particular property type or segment in a primary market. In the 1980s and 1990s, some U.S. major markets had a glut of certain types of space, and you could not find financing for that property type in those markets. Much of this was caused by the wide availability of capital and speculative building, such as large office buildings with no tenants to occupy the space. One building may be absorbed quickly, but when many buildings are added to a specific market all at one time, leasing the space becomes very difficult and hence the funds available to finance this product type become very scarce.

2. Property type—As mentioned previously, the commercial properties that have the most readily available financing are retail, office, industrial, and multifamily (apartments; see Figure 11.1), sometimes known as the four major food groups. In the mid-2000s, flagged hotels became known as the fifth major food group. *Flagged* refers to the franchise or reservation system with which the hotel is associated, for instance, Holiday Inn is the Intercontinental Hotel Group (IHG), and Hampton Inn is from the Hilton Hotel Group. (Figure 11.2 shows a typical non-flagged hotel/motel.) Another property type is mobile home parks (MHP), which were some of the most difficult properties to finance for years. Then they became one of the most sought-after property types for lenders to finance because of the consistency of cash flow, barriers to entry for new competitive properties, and consistently high occupancy. MHPs can still be financed with many lenders at extremely attractive (low) interest rates.

3. Property quality—Newer properties that will attract tenants and customers for future years are more attractive to lenders

Figure 11.1 Typical Class A Apartment or Multifamily Property

for many reasons. They are easier to retenant if leases expire or current tenants move out of their space. Also, there should be less capital expenditure cost during the term of the loan, which leaves more money for the borrower to pay debt service and more cash flow to the borrower. Buildings that are considered green, meaning they are more efficient and less harmful to the environment, are also becoming popular and may help in lender pricing considerations.

4. Credit quality—The quality of the tenant or tenants has a substantial impact on lender pricing for office proper- ties, industrial properties, and retail projects. Better quality is typically defined by Moody's (http://www.moodys.com) and Standard & Poor's (http://www.standardandpoors.com) as investment grade according to ratings such as A, AA, AAA, B, BB, and BBB+. Both services charge to review corporate rat- ings and can be accessed from the Internet. They rate several hundred thousand companies. The reason this is important is that the better the credit quality of the tenant, the less risk of the tenant vacating the space prior to lease termination and the less risk of the tenant going out of business. And because the income of the tenant is used to pay the monthly debt ser- vice (interest) to the lender, that equates to less risk to the lender.

5. Borrower strength and experience—A borrower's experience and high net worth usually help to obtain better pricing. Although the lender is really looking first toward the prop- erty for repayment of the loan and then to the borrower, a substantial borrower helps the lender's credit and pricing decisions. Even with a nonrecourse loan, in which the bor- rower can simply walk away from the loan and property with no recourse from the borrower, lenders like borrowers with

higher net worth. The theory is that in the event the property needs capital improvements or goes through a rough patch, the borrower can feed the property and fund those property needs.

6. Property location—Back to the old adage: location, location, location. If the property is very well located, the lender can be confident that the property should always be well occupied and be able to service the debt adequately through the term of the loan and also readily refinanced with another lender at the end of the loan term. Location also includes how the property is situated on the site and the ease of access to the property. For instance, a retail project is best situated if it is parallel to the street, not perpendicular. Other considerations include whether the property is on what is called the going home side of the street.

7. Loan to value request—The aggressiveness or conservativeness of the loan request also affects the pricing. The higher the loan request as a percentage of value, the more risk to the lender, so they may charge a higher interest rate to reward them for this additional risk. Most lenders lend at a level of 75 percent of the value of the property as a standard practice. Many lenders are prohibited from exceeding this level because of federal constraints (U.S. banks), internal guidelines (life insurance companies), or secondary market buyers (CMBS/conduit lenders). In most cases, lenders quote a 75 percent loan interest rate, but when you are requesting a substantially lower loan amount, such as a 50 percent or 60 percent loan, in many cases you can persuade the lender to be more aggressive in the interest rate or some other terms of the loan. In many cases, you can request a nonrecourse or limited-recourse loan from a typically recourse lender, or

you can request a period of interest-only payments during the initial period of the loan term.

8. Term and amortization request—You can usually achieve a lower interest rate for your client with a shorter loan term and a shorter amortization period. The shorter term is usually priced based on a lower index, such as the 5-year U.S. Treasury versus the 10-year U.S. Treasury. The shorter amortization indicates that the loan is being repaid faster, and in the case of a non-fully-amortizing loan, the balance will be much lower at the end of the term. A 30-year mortgage will have amortized or repaid only about 15 percent of the principal after 10 years. In this case, if the market had declined, then the refinance or exit strategy may be difficult. Conversely, if the loan was amortized over 20 years, 33 percent of the principal would have been repaid after 10 years, and in the event of a 15-year amortization, 45 percent of the principal will be repaid after 10 years.

As I have mentioned many times in this book, all lenders are not created equal. With this in mind, you must consider all eight items and which of these items are most important to which lenders. The most important thing you must remember when representing your client to obtain the most attractive financing for a commercial property is to send the deal to the best lender for the property type. Some lenders fund only on credit retail projects, so sending them a loan that does not fit in their box is not a good use of your time or the lender's time. In fact, a lender could get annoyed if you continually send them deals that they have no interest in financing. Lenders have been known to change focus occasionally as well, so it is important to keep in touch with your lender pool on a regular basis to know what they are looking for and if their focus has changed.

Lessons Learned

I was looking for financing for a hotel property that was situated on an unsubordinated ground lease in a very good location. I had run out of lenders and ideas when I got a call from a lender I hadn't talked to for several months. We talked for a minute, and he said he was in Santa Fe where the property for the hotel was located. I said I had just been there working on a hotel loan. I told him about the loan request and he said, "Tell me more." Within 60 days, I was picking up a $39,000 origination fee check, and this was a property type that this lender had *not* considered in the past. I was about to give up, and that is why you have to keep in constant communication with all of your lenders.

DOCUMENTS ASSOCIATED WITH LENDER TERM QUOTES AND LOCKING THE INTEREST RATE

1. Loan application: Some lenders issue this when they are ready to move forward with a loan.
2. Term sheet: Some lenders issue this before or instead of a loan application.
3. Quote sheet: In the event the lender gives you a verbal quote first to determine if the borrower is interested, you will need to issue this to convey the lender quote to the potential borrower.
4. Multilender quote sheet: In the event you speak to multiple lenders about a loan, you may want to issue one of these.

Figure 11.2   Typical Non-Flagged Hotel/Motel Property

5. Locking the interest rate: Some lenders automatically lock the interest at the issuance and acceptance of the loan application. Some lenders lock the rate three days before closing, and some lock only with a good faith deposit that will be returned at closing.

6. Loan commitment: This is issued by the lender once the loan is approved by lender's committee.

Chapter 12

How Loans Get Closed and Funded—and How You Get Paid

The typical deal takes about 60 days from loan application to loan closing and funding. The standard time periods are 30 days for loan approval and then an additional 30 days for documentation and funding. During the loan approval period, the lender reviews all the items in the final loan submission outlined in Chapter 10. The loan officer prepares a write-up or loan recommendation for the lender's loan committee that includes sections on the borrower's experience and background, the borrower's financial position, the property, the location, the market, the tenants in the property, and potential risks in the financing. Once the loan is approved, the lender issues a loan commitment to fund the loan, which is subject to the receipt of acceptable reports that are to be completed by outside third parties. In most cases, these third-party reports are ordered after the loan is approved by the lender, so the borrower does not incur these costs prior to knowing if the loan has been approved. Some lenders order these reports prior to approval and proceed down parallel paths of approval and closing because these reports are needed before loan approval. With these lenders, your borrower will not receive a formal loan commitment until just days before closing, if they receive one at all.

Depending on the lender and if you are a correspondent for the particular lender with whom you are working, you will be responsible for all or only some of the following steps in the approval and closing process.

1. Loan commitment: Once the loan is approved, you will receive a loan commitment from the lender. You are responsible for reviewing the terms in the loan commitment to be sure they are in agreement with the terms on the loan application the borrower executed. The loan commitment supersedes the loan application, so any changes from the original loan

141

application need to be pointed out to the borrower. You are being paid by the borrower to represent them with the lender. You are then responsible for taking the loan commitment to the borrower and reviewing it with them in person and having them execute the commitment. Normally, the lender requires an additional good faith deposit from the borrower to be returned with the commitment. The deposit is typically 1 percent to 2 percent of the loan amount and is refunded at the time of loan funding. This deposit is to keep the borrower from walking away from the loan commitment after the lender has expended so much time to get to that point in the transaction.

Lesson Learned

I was a broker in an office early in my career when another broker did not closely review the lender loan commitment. The commitment had changed the prepayment language from the step-down, fixed-percentage prepay that was in the loan application to a yield maintenance, which is much less desirable. The broker did not notice and, anxious to get closer to his fee, encouraged the borrower to execute the commitment. He signed the document, and no one noticed until the draft loan documents were issued and being reviewed by the borrower's attorney. The borrower threatened to sue everyone and refused to move forward with the financing. Finally, the lender agreed to go back to the original structure and avoid the aggravation of unwinding the whole loan. It was clear that the lender did not have to make that concession, and the borrower was bound to the commitment he executed.

---

2. Loan documents: The lender or the lender's in-house counsel or outside counsel will prepare the loan documents based on the terms outlined in the loan commitment. Typically, the lender will provide a set of draft loan documents for the borrower to review. I recommend that you always suggest that the borrower have his own legal counsel review at least the major loan documents, such as the promissory note and mortgage or deed of trust. A typical set of loan documents are as follows:

   A. Promissory note: This is the document that outlines the monetary terms of the loan—interest rate, loan amount, payments and due dates, prepayment restrictions, default interest, late charges, and due on sale clauses.

   B. Mortgage or deed of trust: This document outlines more of the security items, covenants the borrower has to maintain the property and maintain insurance, payment of taxes, lease requirements, annual reporting documents that the borrower has to provide to the borrower at the end of each year, default provisions, notice and cure rights, due on sale or encumbrance language, permitted interparty transfers, governing law language, and redemption period language.

   C. Guarantee: In the event the loan is guaranteed in whole or in part by the borrower, the borrower will execute this separate agreement defining the parameter of the guarantee.

   D. Tenant estoppel: This is the document that the tenants sign, outlining all the terms of the lease with each tenant. These are prepared by the borrower or by the mortgage broker on the lender's form from the information contained in the lease. The tenant then signs the estoppel, which verifies the terms of the lease. In the event there are amendments not provided by the borrower to the lender, this is where the lender is able to determine that they have received and reviewed and underwritten the full and complete lease.

These documents are not recorded at the county recording office.

E. Tenant subordination and nondisturbance agreement: These are recorded documents that allow for the new loan to become superior to the existing leases, which then become subordinate to the loan. This document also acknowledges that in the event of a foreclosure, the lender will not disturb or terminate the tenants' leases and lease rights.

F. Assignment of lessor's interest in leases: This is executed by the borrower and, in the event of a foreclosure, assigns all rights of the borrower or landlord to the lender or lender's assignee.

G. Insurance and/or tax impound letter: Many lenders impound and pay taxes and insurance on behalf of the borrower. In many cases, the lender will agree to waive the impound until or unless the borrower pays his mortgage late one or more times in a 12-month period, at which time the lender can begin to impound for taxes and insurance.

H. W-9: This is to verify to whom the loan proceeds are given and who is paying the tax-deductible interest for tax purposes.

I. Spousal consent form: This document is an acknowledgment that both husband and wife are aware of the impending indebtedness in community property states or with jointly owned property when both husband and wife are not executing the loan documents.

J. Borrower's counsel opinion letter: This is written by the borrower's attorney, using the lender's form, opining that the loan and loan documents are legal and enforceable in the state where the property is located.

K. Settlement or HUD statement: A document prepared by the title company showing all income and costs of the loan and to whom items are to be paid.

L. Closing letter to title company from lender: This letter is written by the lender outlining under which conditions the title company will be permitted to release the loan proceeds to the borrower.

3. Third-party reports: The typical third-party reports are the property appraisal, the phase 1 environmental report, the property condition report, and in the case of a multifamily (apartment complex), a termite inspection.

A. The appraisal is ordered by either the lender or the mortgage banker, but never by the borrower. I typically contact three acceptable appraisal firms, provide them with the specifics of my underwriting and details of the property, and ask them if they can complete the appraisal, how long it will take to complete, and what the cost will be. I then give the options of timing and cost information to the borrower and ask them if they are acceptable or else I just engage the one that can complete the appraisal the quickest for the least amount of money. It is also important to get an indication that they feel the required property value is achievable based on the preliminary information provided. The appraisal engagement letter is either provided by the appraiser or drafted by the broker or lender. Most lenders of loans in excess of $500,000 will require an appraisal with three approaches to value:

1. The Income approach, which uses the income of the property and divides it by a capitalization rate to arrive at a value. The capitalization rate is determined by what a buyer is willing to pay for a property or the return they

are willing to receive as a percentage of the purchase price. The capitalization rate for a very safe investment such as a Walgreen's store would be low, in the 6 percent range, meaning that a buyer would be willing to accept a lower return because of the lower risk associated with the high quality of the Walgreen's tenant.

2. The sales approach, which is basically determined by the value or purchase price expressed as a per square foot amount. For example, a class A office building may sell for $150 to $200 per square foot. So if the building contains 10,000 square feet of space, the value would be in $1.5 million to $ million dollars. This is the only approach that can typically be used for vacant land.

3. The Cost Approach or Replacement Cost Approach, which is based on the cost to replace the building if you had to rebuild or replace using today's costs, but depreciated for the age of the structure. This is the least preferred method, especially with the constantly changing costs with the world economy.

B. The phase 1 report primarily records a search of the existing property and if there has been any environmental contamination at the site, as well as any environmental issues with the surrounding sites and if those sites could have contaminated the subject site. These reports normally also include any available historical aerial photos of previous property uses. If there is an indication that there has been any environmental contamination, the lender may require additional testing, known as a phase 2 environmental report. This is a process that requires actual soil samples to be taken from the property and analyzed for any environmental contamination. They actually drill holes into the subject ground and pull up soil samples to analyze.

C. The property condition report (PCR) or property condition assessment (PCA) is a report for which an engineer inspects the property structure, roofs, mechanical components (HVAC), parking lot asphalt condition, and the entire buildings, units, and property. This report identifies any deferred maintenance that needs to be completed, as well as the economic life of the roof, HVAC, and other components and outlines current and future capital expenditure needs.

4. Termite inspection: Most multifamily lenders require a termite inspection report. In the event there is evidence of termites, the lender will require all areas to be sprayed and an ongoing maintenance plan to be put in place.

5. The survey: Most lenders today do not require a survey, as long as the title company will remove the survey or zoning exception from the title policy. In other words, the title company gives title insurance to the lender that covers zoning and property encroachments. Some lenders, usually on larger loans, require a new survey to be completed and certified to the lender so they can rely on its accuracy. The lender compares the survey with all easements and the like to the recorded title documents described next.

6. Title commitment and title policy: The lender initially requires a preliminary title report that lists all documents recorded against the property. They also need to review the actual underlying documents that are recorded on the property, as outlined in schedule B of the title report. The title company also prepares a title commitment that outlines the title condition or state of title that will exist after the funding of the

loan. For example, it may show the new loan in first position and the existing loan removed as it will be paid off from the new loan. Other items that show up on title may be mechanics' liens if work had been recently completed at the property or in the event of a construction loan. The borrower will be responsible for obtaining lien releases for these liens. Easements also show up on the title and on the survey. Easements are access to the property granted to another party, such as a utility easement in which electrical power may run to or across the property. These can run underground or above ground, and the building structure cannot encroach on these easements.

The closing process should almost be a rubber stamp if you have done all things correctly to this point. The loan documents should have been reviewed and negotiated, the third-party reports all reviewed and approved, and the cost of the transactions should have been reviewed by both parties so there are no surprises. The one item that always seems to become an issue is the closing costs of the loan. You should be sure that all parties have reviewed some sort of HUD or settlement statement prior to going to final loan signing. If a borrower is not prepared to see a $15,000 legal fee on the statement, I guarantee you will get an earful. I have been in many closings where the borrower threatened not to close if the legal fees weren't reduced or at least split with the broker. So be prepared when you are dealing with those lenders who use outside legal counsel to prepare and negotiate their loan documents.

YOUR RESPONSIBILITIES AFTER THE LOAN CLOSES

Once the loan closes and funds, you as the mortgage broker or mortgage banker may have ongoing responsibilities to the lender. If you are a correspondent for the lender, you will certainly have all or some of the responsibilities outlined here. Completing these ongoing responsibilities after the loan has closed is referred to as servicing the loan. Many large residential and commercial mortgage bankers service the loans they originate for the lenders they represent in the marketplace.

Servicing: Ongoing monitoring of the loan on behalf of the lender. Lenders typically pay their correspondents for performing this work. The standard payment is five basis points of the loan amount per year. One hundred basis points is equal to 1 percent. Five basis points is equal to five one-hundredths of 1 percent paid per year. For example, on a $1 million loan, a 1 percent fee is $10,000, and you divide that by 20 to get to the annual payment of $500. That isn't very much on its own, but if you have a servicing portfolio of $1 billion, the annual fee could be $500,000. Many mortgage banking firms split the commission between the firm and the individual producer/mortgage banker at a higher level for loans that the firm will service versus loans they will not service. To begin servicing loans for a lender, you need to establish a consistent relationship with that lender and have completed a number of transactions with them.

Treasury versus non treasury servicing: Many lenders used to incorporate what they referred to as treasury functions as part of the servicing completed by the mortgage banker. Treasury functions mean that the mortgage banker actually collected the monthly payments on behalf of the lender and deposited them or forwarded them to the lender as the agent for the lender. This could be beneficial to the borrower because once the payment was received by the mortgage company, it would be considered received by the lender, and if the property was located in the same city as the mortgage company, the borrower could just drop the payment off on the due date and not have to worry about the mail or overnight delivery service. Many lenders today have moved to an automatic clearing house (ACH) procedure in which the lender's bank automatically drafts the monthly interest payment on the date agreed to in the promissory note. One of the biggest negotiation points in all deals is when the payment is due. For an apartment complex where the borrower has many tenants and needs all the rent checks received and deposited to pay the monthly interest, and those payments are due on the fifth day of each month, which is the same day the interest payment is drafted, it can become an issue for the borrower. Many lenders allow the due date to be moved to the tenth when there are many tenants. Other lenders, however, may never give in on that negotiation.

Property inspections and annual documentation: This is the function that is most common in today's servicing requirements by the lending community. Most lenders have annual reporting requirements for the borrower. Typically at the end of each calendar year, within 90 days of that time, the borrower must furnish the lender with current financial information relating to the property. This information normally includes a current rent roll and the previous year's operating statement or profit and loss statement. They may also require personal financial information on the borrower, such as an updated personal financial statement and most recent tax return. What is required depends on the type of lender and loan and if the loan is recourse or guaranteed by the borrower. In the case of conduit loans, the lenders require the borrower to submit monthly information on the property for the first year or until the time that the loan is securitized and sold off in the market place. After the sale, the reporting is on an annual basis. The mortgage broker is responsible for obtaining this information annually from the borrower if they are in the capacity of servicing the loan. This may seem like an easy responsibility, but it is sometimes very difficult to get this information from the borrower once the loan is funded. While not furnishing this information could put the loan in default, it is referred to as a nonmonetary default, meaning it does not have to do with nonpayment of principal and interest, so it is questionable whether the lender could even foreclose for this default.

Annual property inspections include a photograph and comments on the condition of the property, apparent occupancy of the property, and anything else worth noting to the lender. Other items may include new construction in the area or changes in access to the property.

Chapter 13

Anatomy of a Deal

This is the anatomy of the steps taken and the time line of a $2 million refinance loan I recently closed in the Southwest. I thought it would be interesting to share with you the steps and time lines that went into the process.

Day 1. I received a call from a real estate broker with whom I work quite often regarding one of his clients who wanted to refinance a single-tenant office property that the broker had sold him a few years before. These calls typically have the broker explaining the highlights of the deal and may or may not have the proposed borrower on the phone. In this instance the broker had sold the property years before, which is not often the case unless the broker keeps a good, ongoing relationship with his or her borrowers (which is a good practice for us all). The more common call would be from a broker with a current client looking to buy a property in which the broker is involved in the sale. In either event, this is when your information-gathering process begins. Take notes and then ask the broker for any old or current information or the sales package the broker has on the property. These packages often contain information you will want to put in your preliminary and final loan submission to the lender and will also use in your initial underwriting of the deal.

In this particular situation, the broker had the borrower on the phone with us so I was able to become acquainted with him and get his direct contact information. We talked a little about what he was looking to accomplish, and I told him I would call him later when I was back in the office to get his e-mail address to send him a list of items I would need to start the process. This is the reason I always keep my office phone forwarded to my cell phone when I am out of the office. If the call had gone to voice mail I would have missed the opportunity to allow the broker to introduce me to this new client.

Day 2. I drove by the property to kick the tires. You can very often determine if you can finance a property and how easy or difficult it will be simply by visiting/inspecting the property. You want to drive by the subject property and drive through the neighborhood and submarket, taking notes on neighboring properties, construction, competitors, and so on. In addition, take pictures of the subject property, access, neighborhood, and anything else you may think is pertinent to your deal.

The property looked great and very financeable. I then called the proposed borrower and gave him a list of items we would need to obtain the initial loan quotes. This information is, at a minimum: rent roll (or, even better, the actual leases that I would use to prepare my own rent roll), operating history, property information/description, borrower resume, and any type of old appraisal that I can use to better understand the submarket of the property. The full list would include tax returns on the principals, borrowers, and property; personal financial statements; borrowing entity organization documents; all leases; site plan; and a preliminary title report; but I didn't need all that for an initial loan quote. It would be nice to receive everything up front, but in most cases borrowers do not want to send out their personal financial information unless they know they have an acceptable loan quote.

I also called the broker and asked him to forward any marketing or other information he had on the property.

Day 3. I received the single-tenant lease from the broker, read the lease, and began my underwriting using the rental and expense information from the lease.

Days 4 and 5. I waited for additional information from the borrower and worked on other loans and deals.

Day 6. I received the minimal information I requested from the borrower: the historical operating statements (income and expenses) on the property, a hard copy of the lease, a brief resume on the borrower and borrowing entity, and a description of the property. In addition, I had a detailed conversation with the borrower in which he outlined what he was looking to accomplish with the refinancing. It is important not to hear that a borrower wants a 10-year loan based on a 30-year amortization at a low interest rate. I always drill down further to determine why someone is refinancing and what his or her long-term business plan is for the property. You need to know this when looking for the loan quotes. For instance, if the borrower plans to pay off the loan within two years, you need to make the sure there are no prepayment penalties or talk to him or her about a shorter-term loan.

I now had the financial information on the property—lease(s) and historical operating information—to complete my initial underwriting. After driving by the property and submarket (or reviewing photographs of the property if it is not in your immediate market area), the initial underwriting or economic analysis is the most important step. This is the analysis of the income, value of the property, and cash flow available to pay debt service (principal and interest) from the property. The final value and determination of these items will come from the appraisal (which in some cases will be further adjusted by the lender), but you need to complete an initial analysis to be sure that what the borrower is requesting in loan terms is achievable or at least in the ballpark of what is achievable (see the previous chapter on underwriting). I completed my analysis based on the terms (capitalization rate, market vacancy, management cost, etc.) that I thought were appropriate for the property and market, and concluded that the request was achievable and did not appear to be a full loan request. This was great news.

The next step was to move this deal to the top of the pile. I often receive calls on deals with "what if?" types of questions. When I get one of those calls and then obtain the follow-up information that supports the loan request, I move quickly to put some quotes on the table so I can get the deal off the street. There is always competition on deals, and by moving more quickly and delivering a quote that meets the borrower's expectations you can eliminate that competition by getting the deal signed up with you, thereby taking it off the street from other brokers that may be looking at it.

During this short period, I did two things simultaneously. I had a good idea of what the deal was about, so I identified three lenders and made calls to those three lenders. I spoke to them in general terms about the deal and asked if they had an interest in quoting on the loan opportunity. I also finished my preliminary submission with the plan to send it to any lenders I was able to speak with the same day. After completing the preliminary submission, I waited to hear back from my lenders. I called the borrower and told him that I had calls in to three lenders and should have loan quotes in one to two days.

Day 7. All three lenders called back, and two of the three had an interest in the deal. I sent the preliminary package to those two lenders. I was comfortable with their level of interest, so I did not call any additional lenders at that point.

One of the two remaining lenders called back with a loan quote. I asked the lender to send me an e-mail or fax outlining this soft loan quote. I immediately called the borrower and outlined the terms under which the lender would be interested in pursing the loan opportunity.

Day 8. The second lender provided a loan quote, which I immediately conveyed to the borrower. Based on my experience I was able to inform the borrower that these two quotes were indeed indicative of the market of lenders with whom I worked. The first loan quote met his requirements and was more attractive than the second loan quote, so the borrower told me to move forward with that lender and request a loan application, which would be the next step.

Day 9. I issued the loan application to the borrower and set up a meeting to go over the terms with him in person.

Day 10. We reviewed the loan application, and the borrower signed it and delivered a one-quarter percent good-faith deposit with the executed loan application.

The next step was to prepare a full loan submission for the lender, which would eventually be taken to the lender's loan committee for approval. I prepared a list of items I would need from the borrower to complete this loan submission and went over that list with the borrower. I also completed a rent roll for the borrower to certify and to send back with the requested information. Typically the final loan submission needs to be delivered to the lender within one to two weeks after delivery of the executed loan application.

Day 11. I ordered a preliminary title report from the title company.

Day 15. I received an overnight package from the borrower containing the items I had requested. It was a full package that even included personal financial information from the borrower. In many instances you will receive only the property information on a deal and a brief description of the borrower and his or her financial information. Many borrowers do not want to release personal information until they have been provided a loan quote that meets or comes close to their request. You must learn to work within these parameters, asking for enough information to qualify the borrowers in the event they are unwilling to release the personal information in the initial/preliminary loan submission.

In this case, I did receive a very full package, which included the following six items:

1. Rent roll certified by the borrower. I had e-mailed him a copy I had already prepared so he could print it out and certify it to be true and correct. Many times this is done during the closing process, but again anything you can complete early will make things easier later on.
2. Borrower resume.
3. Borrower personal financial statement.
4. Borrower personal tax returns.
5. Borrowing entity documents.
6. Hard copy of all leases (I had already received the only lease by e-mail).

A site plan or small 8 × 10 survey would have been nice, but since the borrower did not have one I used a close-up aerial view for that purpose until a survey could be obtained.

Day 16. I continued to work on compilation of the final loan submission. I ordered credit reports, aerials, and demographic information. The borrower informed me he would be on vacation for the next 12 days.

Day 17. I completed the full loan submission and submitted it to the lender.

Day 21. The lender called me with questions and requests for clarifications of information contained in the loan submission. The lender also asked for additional information on the submarket of the property pertaining to rental rates and vacancies.

Day 23. I responded with answers to the questions on which I was able to obtain additional information. I asked the lender to approve the loan "subject to" the items I was unable to answer due to my borrower being on vacation.

Day 30. The lender informed me that the loan had been approved and delivered a loan commitment for the borrower to execute.

The typical commercial loan takes 60 days to fund. It is broken down as 30 days for a loan commitment and 30 days to close. This 60-day period typically starts with the issuance of a loan application, not with the initial conversation with the borrower. This transaction moved more quickly than a typical deal for two reasons: first, my quick response to the potential loan request and obtaining the initial loan quotes quickly, and second, the timely turnaround by the borrower of all requested information needed to move to the loan commitment stage.

Day 33. The borrower executed the loan commitment, delivered any additional outstanding items, and deposited the required 2 percent commitment fee and good-faith deposit.

Day 34. I submitted requests to three appraisers for timing and cost to complete the required appraisal on the subject property. I engaged a firm to complete the Phase 1 report and property condition report (if required).

Day 37. I received quotes from the appraisers and reviewed them with the borrower. There is always a trade-off between timing of delivery of the report and cost of the report. The soonest the report could be delivered was in 17 days and the costs were all similar, so I engaged the appraiser with the quickest turnaround. I always share my underwriting with the appraisers so if they think it is not achievable I can address that issue immediately with the lender and appraiser. If they think it is reasonable but need to complete the assignment before they can commit, then that is all I expect at the initial engagement.

Day 40. I worked with the borrower on zoning letters, property insurance, and certificates of good standing for the borrowing entity. The zoning certification letter was ordered from the city.

Day 45. Loan documents were sent to the borrower and borrower's counsel in draft form. In this case, the documents were not negotiable by the borrower, but on larger loans or complex loans the negotiation process could take many weeks.

The Phase 1 report was received and showed no issues. The lender did not require a property condition report.

The lender asked for changes to the insurance certificates and to the title endorsements.

Day 48. The lender approved the Phase 1 report and the form of property insurance provided by the borrower's insurance agent.

Day 52. The certificate of good standing was received from the state's corporation commission.

Day 54. The zoning letter was received from the local city zoning department. I called the appraiser and asked how the report was coming along as it was now due.

Day 57. The appraisal was received. I reviewed the appraisal and then sent it to the lender for review and approval. Most lenders need several days to approve the appraisal. The lender asked for more changes to the title endorsements.

Day 58. The appraisal was accepted and approved by the lender. The title commitment was accepted by the lender.

Day 59. Loan documents were sent to the title company. A closing was set up for the borrower to come in and execute the loan documents.

Day 60. The loan documents that need to be recorded with the county were recorded. The lender funded the money to the title company.

Day 61. I picked up a $21,000 check representing my fee for the transaction.

PART III

Chapter 14

Ethics

Commercial mortgage brokerage is one of the least regulated businesses in the United States today. It is necessary for the people in the business to conduct themselves with common etiquette and high ethical standards. Your reputation is one of the most important sales points of your business. This is not a large community, probably less than a hundredth of the number of residential brokers, who are extensively regulated. You always want to conduct yourself in a manner so that you would not hesitate to give the name and number of one of your previous clients to someone you are approaching for new business.

EXAMPLES OF WHAT IS NOT ACCEPTABLE

In a very competitive business such as this, you will run across brokers who often use the bait-and-switch approach in one of two ways, and neither is an acceptable practice. Sometimes the broker simply lies about the rate he has from a lender to get the borrower to work with him and pushes to have the borrower sign an engagement letter. The broker then tells the borrower that the lender changed the quote from what the lender originally told them. By this time, the borrower is already committed to work with this devious broker and does not walk away. In this case, the broker knew the lender did not quote the terms the broker represented but lied to get the business. Other times, the broker just tells the borrower what they want to hear as to terms, even though the broker has not even talked to any lenders and has no idea what they will ultimately quote on the loan request. In the unlikely event the lender quotes the same quote, the broker says nothing, and in the event the lender quotes less favorable terms, the broker blames the lender, and again there is a high probability that the borrower will stay with this broker.

Another tactic used by some unethical brokers I often run across in my market is the threat of rates going up unless the borrower executes the loan application or loan commitment immediately. I have had many calls from borrowers asking if this threat is accurate, and in most cases there is no validity, except that the other broker is anxious to just get the deal signed up so they don't lose it to another broker.

Remember, your responsibility is to obtain the most favorable financing options for your client, not just to get paid!

Another unethical practice I have seen used is when a borrower approaches the mortgage broker with a financing need and the mortgage broker discourages them and tells their request is impossible or unachievable, and so the borrower moves on to other potential developments or projects. Then the mortgage broker takes the potential borrower's idea and runs with it himself. This could be a new motorcycle or fast-food franchise the borrower wanted to bring to the market, an old shopping center the prospective borrower wanted to buy from an existing institutional investor that no longer wants to own it and then redevelop the center with a new concept, or the borrower was just looking for a construction/permanent loan to develop an apartment complex or Walgreen's store in an area that needed this development.

As the mortgage broker/banker, you must behave as an honorable person, be honest and straightforward, and consider all personal information as confidential.

I have been in the company of other mortgage brokers who would routinely and without hesitation talk freely about their clients' net worth, personal information, and loan terms of properties they had financed for their clients. This is absolutely unacceptable and is sure to prevent you from ever working in this town again if the borrower finds out about this. In addition, would you want to do business with someone who talks about other people they do business with? That broker will surely be talking about your loans and personal information to the public in no time.

I often see that knowing look in real estate brokers' eyes when I tell them I will pay them a referral fee for a lead that comes to fruition and leads to a loan funding. They look as though they have heard the promise many times but have never actually experienced it actually happening, never actually received a referral fee. I paid in excess of $50,000 in referral fees last year. If you say you are going to pay it, then pay it. If you don't want to pay them, then say that as well. In many cases, I offer to pay a referral to a real estate broker and they decline because they are making a commission, and they really are looking to me to be sure the loan closes in the case of an acquisition so that the broker will get paid. Many times the certainty of execution in referring the deal to an experienced, honest, ethical mortgage banker/broker is repaid by the ability of the broker to deliver the required financing so that all parties get paid their respective fees. I have also heard mortgage brokers say something along the lines of "I am not getting in your pocket, so don't get in mine. Let's just both do our jobs, and we will all get paid."

Kickbacks or back-end fees can also be unethical if they are paid to you as a mortgage broker/banker. In the early days of CMBS/conduit lending many supposedly smart brokers starting approaching these lenders to be paid back end fees after the loan was closed. The idea came from the residential mortgage industry, where this was a common practice. At first the lender would just pay the broker part of their fee as additional compensation, but it then evolved to a situation in which the lender would add some number of basis points to the interest rate, which would equate to an additional loan fee that would be paid to the broker, behind the borrower's back. This is actually a process that can be acceptable and preferable in some cases as long as it is disclosed to all parties. For instance, you may have a borrower who is working on a refinance, and he may say to the you as the broker that he would like a par deal, meaning that he would not pay a fee to you directly, but it would be paid by the lender and included in the loan interest rate. Again, as long as this is all disclosed to all parties, it can be an acceptable practice, but it is rarely used by most of the brokerage community.

Remember, you are always selling yourself in this business, and your ability to find your client the most attractive financing to fit their needs and your reputation and ethics will play a very large part in achieving that goal with both your clients and your lenders.

Chapter 15

Advanced Strategies for Taking Your Business to the Next Level

Once you have brokered a number of loans and have experience, you may want to consider some of the following methods to ramp up your business and increase your income.

1. *Joint ventures:* Take your fee in equity in the project rather than as a fee up front. In larger deals, this is much more likely to be available. Rather than the borrower paying you a 1 percent fee, you may be able to become a limited partner in the project and own 2 percent to 5 percent of the project.

2. *Partner with a bank or bridge lender:* Lenders who want only 6- to 18-month projects are known as bridge or short-term or redevelopment lenders. You can sign an agreement with one of these lenders that allows you to look at all of their loans when they are ready to mature so the lender will have an exit strategy and the borrower will have a source for a longer-term, lower-rate loan. You may even want to underwrite the loans at the beginning of the process when the bridge lender is making the initial loan, which will help all parties: The lender will know they have a take-out/exit strategy, the borrower will know they have access to longer-term financing at better rates when the project is complete, and you have just earned yourself a future deal and a future paycheck.

3. *Referrals:* Pay a percentage or a flat amount. Go out and solicit business from others and agree to pay them a referral fee if they send you a loan. If it is a deal that you would not have otherwise been aware of, then it is worth it to you to pay them a fee. I usually pay between 10 percent and 25 percent of my fee. More than 25 percent does not make economic sense for me unless it is a larger deal, in which case I have just split the fee fifty-fifty.

4. *Write a newsletter or e-zine:* These can be extremely effective for the real estate brokerage community. If you are consistent, they will absolutely bring in calls on new deals. If you are using e-mail, you want to get the permission of the recipient. You want to make your communication very simple, not too busy. You want to include these items: (1) where your lender rates are today on 5-year, 10-year, 15-year, and 20-year commercial deals; (2) a box that shows what the major indexes—the 10-year U.S. Treasury, 30- or 90-day LIBOR, prime, and the 10-year swap rate—are doing; (3) a tombstone of one or two deals you recently funded; (4) highlighting one of the lenders you represent, outlining the deals they focus on, where they are headquartered, recent deals they have funded, annual volume, and loan parameters; and (5) upcoming events, such as a Federal Reserve meeting, upcoming jobs growth reports, or upcoming earnings reports of major U.S. companies, such as Wal-Mart.

5. *Seminars:* Host seminars for large real estate brokerage firms at their office, in their conference rooms. Talk to the head of the firm and schedule it with them. Tell them you want to discuss the current lending environment, where lenders get their money (a little history lesson), where your rates are today, what kind of deals you are looking for, and what kind of turnaround time they can expect from quote to closing. You can also host a large seminar for, say, residential mortgage brokers at one of the local hotels.

6. *Conferences:* Attend some national lending conferences. The largest would be the annual Commercial Real Estate Finance (CREF) Conference, hosted by the Mortgage Bankers Association. This is an excellent event for meeting new lenders. There are open and closed sessions, and this is an opportunity

to start or add to your lender pool. Schedule as many meetings as you can, and ask for every business card you can carry. Even if you only get a card, you can call them and talk about a deal when you are back at your office. No one really remembers who they meet, but if you call them with a deal and use the approach in this book, you will have a new lender! CREF is held once a year, Superbowl weekend, in either Orlando, Florida, or San Diego, California. There are also many other lending conferences you can attend, and many of them are more focused on specific property types such as hotels or apartments/multifamily.

7. *Direct mail pieces:* This is a commonly used approach and I think a good one. I always read all the postcard type of mailers I receive. I honestly do scan every one. I receive a lot from lenders about deals they have funded or current terms and property types. I called from one recently and funded a loan with that lender within 60 days and was paid a fee. If I scan them, I think most people do, and with a postcard, if something grabs them, they will give you a quick call about their property. You only have that one day to connect with them. You have to answer that call the first time or return that call the same day; if not, they will have gone on to another business. If you do connect with them the same day, you have already passed the question about credibility that comes standard with all postcard mailers. Focus these cards on owners and developers, but you can include real estate brokers.

8. *Lists for sale:* There are many lists available for all types of customers and clients. You can use these lists for letters outlining who you are and what you do. They are valuable for marketing to owner-occupied property owners.

9. *Commercial real estate brokers:* They can be one of the most valuable sources of business you can cultivate. These people are driven solely by the sales commission, and if you can help that happen by finding a good loan for their buyer and making the transaction happen in a timely manner, then they will bring every deal they can to you.

10. *Residential mortgage brokers:* Also a great source for business, these brokers already understand much of the business and are already with a client and have access to their financial information. If the brokers see their client also owns a commercial property, they can ask them if they are interested in financing that property as well. They can call you for a soft loan quote and pass it on to the borrower, or they can bring you in to meet with the borrower. This a great source for business, as long as they haven't already bought this book and are making commercial loans on their own.

11. *Property managers:* Property managers should be a great source of business for you. They pay the bills of the property, know the existing mortgage information, and are focused on cutting costs and keeping expenses low for the owner. If you told them you could lower their monthly mortgage by several thousand dollars or more, they should be knocking down you and the owner's doors to get you together. This is one of the simplest ways to cut costs on *any* property! Get a list of the large and small management companies in your area, and set up meetings with the owners and managers. This marketing needs to be done face to face, not with a mailing.

12. *Title companies:* Stay in touch with active title company title and escrow officers. They oversee a lot of loan closings and work with a lot of owners and developers. It is too late for the deal they are closing now (unless it is a construction or

bridge loan), but if they know what rates you are quoting, they may give your name to their client or give their client's name to you. This is a great way to find new business and active borrowers.

13. *Accountants:* They have many of the same assets as the property managers.

14. *Existing customers:* It is important to keep in touch with all of your past clients. They need to be thinking of you first whenever they're thinking about a new deal. Believe me, your competition is marketing to them all the time, so you should be as well.

15. *Thank you after the loan closes:* This ties into the last suggestion. You need to stay in front of your clients, keep them happy, and even ask them if they were happy with the job you did for them. Also ask them if there is anything you could have done differently (within your control) to make the deal smoother. Along the same lines, you should set up a database of everyone you have worked with on a loan that closed. This needs to be separate from your larger Outlook or Act database. You want to be able to access these names quickly so you can stay in front of them and ask for future business. These clients are also potential clients to buy other properties in your market that you can finance.

16. *Expand into other markets:* Find another market that does not have a lot of competition where you think you can be successful. It should be an underserved market for your type of lenders, a market dominated by the local banks. This move will require a lot of follow-up so clients know you will be around. You will also want to get a local phone number, mailing address, and business cards. You can use a local UPS mailbox center for the address. Try to get a box with a number

that sounds like an office, like #101 or #301. This shows commitment to the new market, which is important because borrowers don't want to start a new relationship with a new lender that may disappear next month. You need to really be consistent in your marketing and calls as well.

17. *Cold calls:* This can be focused to property owners near and around the area where you recently closed a loan. Send a card with a picture or tombstone of the recently closed deal, and talk about looking for more business in that submarket. It is much easier to market after already closing a loan in the area because it adds more credibility to your ability to deliver a loan.

18. *Business cards and elevators:* Always have business cards with you, and perfect your elevator pitch. An elevator pitch is telling someone what you do in three sentences or less—the time it takes to ride between floors in an elevator. You should practice this and use it often.

Chapter 16

How to Find the Niche That Will Make You Rich!

Here are insider tips and tricks on all different property types—what to look for that is good and bad and what to look out for to focus on.

The four major food groups—office, general retail, industrial, and apartments/multifamily—all have specialties within them that you can make your niche. One of the major things I see and I even find myself doing is mortgage brokers/bankers who jump around to all different types of properties and try to fund every deal put in front of them. Think about all the lenders you may call for one specific deal. On each one of those calls, you learn more about what that lender is trying to accomplish and what they look for in a certain property type. With retail for an example, some lenders may focus on multitenant, some single tenant, some on shadow anchors where the project is located next to an anchor tenant with a big draw of customers, some only strip retail on major thoroughfares, some only on investment-grade quality tenants, and the list goes on. If all these calls and homework took you one to two weeks until you finally talked to all the lenders on your list for this retail loan you are seeking—that's a lot of time! Now you get the loan under application and moving toward approval and closing. It is time to get your next deal in process, if you don't have another deal sitting on your desk, so you need to find a loan (see Chapter 5). Wouldn't it make sense to focus on another deal similar to the deal on which you are currently working? You just spent between one and three weeks finding your lenders for that retail deal, so another retail deal would make the most sense.

This doesn't mean that you should turn down deals that aren't that property type; in fact, in some markets you cannot afford to turn down any deals. A mortgage broker in my market told me once, "I don't see that many deals, so when I get one I work it until I am successful or there are no more lenders to talk to." This is also focus. Once you get in the business, you will start to understand which deals are going to be easy to fund and which requests could become a career deal. Then the difficulty becomes how to say no to a potential borrower. Or take the philosophy that you will call a maximum of four lenders, and if you cannot find a home for the loan, then you will move onto the next loan request. You need to be polite and straightforward with the borrower, something like "Unfortunately, none of my lenders are making competitive loans on that property type today. I don't want either of us to waste too much time when another broker might be able to help you." If you approach that correctly, you still may see another loan request from that borrower. Of course, we are always concerned that the next broker will do a good job, precluding you from seeing a future deal. That is one way to look at it, but if you found two more deals during the month you would have spent on that one deal, you are ahead of the game. Now, this all could be overruled by the large loan request. Everyone is always working on a $30 million to $100 million loan in the background. That helps your mental outlook with the potential of it coming to fruition, but not in place of your focus.

Now let's look at some niche specialties.

Multitenant office properties: The biggest concerns with office properties are the rollover risk and retenant cost when a tenant's lease expires and the tenant vacates the property. A large issue with lender loan underwriting in the 1990s was the rising costs of tenant improvements of office space and whether the property cash flow would be sufficient to pay for that cost. For example, if you are working on a 100,000-square-foot office building with a 20,000-square-foot lease expiring, the cost to complete the tenant improvements to entice a new tenant to move into that vacant space could be $50 to $100 per square foot or $1 million to $2 million.

The owners will also pay a broker the leasing commissions to find the tenant. Where does this money come from? It comes from a reserve account set up at closing, the borrower, or property cash flow. You need to focus on this rollover risk when underwriting office properties. Rollover is when the leases expire or roll, and then the space will, we hope, roll over to a new tenant. In addition to the cost for the new tenant to be put in place, you also need to find a tenant to take that space.

Medical office buildings: These office buildings specialize in medical tenants, who usually have higher water and power needs and because of that can be costlier to build and to retenant.

Single-tenant office properties: All the risks from multitenant properties are present, plus the fact that if you lose only one tenant, you have zero income. With this in mind, you need to really focus on the strength of the tenant and the market. You also want to keep the loan amortization term shorter so the loan is being repaid more rapidly. You may even want to consider a fully amortizing loan that is coterminous with the lease of the tenant. This means the loan matures at the same time as the lease expires.

Strip center retail: This is fairly straightforward real estate. If the lender funds retail loans, then they should be fine with this property type. The things to consider are location, lease rollover, and access. Most lenders like them on busy thoroughfares with good access and parallel to the street so you can see all tenants from the street.

Big box retail: These larger stores range from 25,000 square feet to in excess of 100,000 square feet. A center with numerous big boxes, such as a Best Buy, Linens N Things, Toys R US, Michaels, and Barnes & Noble, is considered a power center. The concern here is the location. The tenants typically sign 10-year leases, so there are retenanting concerns, as well as rollover risks. Another concern is that the rents the tenants pay are usually flat for the term of the lease, while expenses typically increase, so you want to be sure the expenses and the increases are being passed through to the tenant.

Regional malls: Again, many lenders really like to finance this property type. The focus on these properties is on the direction of the city's growth. I have worked on a number of deals in which the city had simply grown away from the mall. These properties rely on the "majors" to bring in customers who must walk through and past all the other stores in the mall, which is an opportunity for them to attract customers they may not otherwise be able to reach. As a focus or niche it is good in that you can get your arms around the handful of lenders financing these properties easily, but that also means that the owners can easily identify these lenders as well so may be less willing to pay you for something they can do themselves.

Freestanding restaurants: The biggest concern with this type of property is that it is a very special use property. If the tenant lease expires or the tenant vacates the space, the pool of replacement tenants is smaller than for other retail uses. In addition, the cost of tenant improvements is typically much higher for a restaurant than for a typical retail storefront, and so if you decide to convert a restaurant to normal multitenant retail, you will have to tear out the existing improvements, which will cost you money, and the value will most likely drop because the replacement retail tenants will pay much less in rent than the restaurant. Finally, most restaurants make poor strip retail centers. For these reasons, the restaurants tend to stay vacant longer than other retail uses. Of course, if the location is strong enough, the re-leasing period should be shorter. Many lenders specialize in restaurant lending. You and the lender will also look closely at whether it is a corporate-owned or franchise store. And if it is a corporate store, how many stores does the company have, and how financially strong are they? You will ask the same questions of the franchise store owner who would be the operator tenant.

Hotels: This is one of the most difficult and profitable niches you can find. The inner circle of this property type is very difficult to break into and to place these loans on a consistent basis. In the past few years, hotels started to become the fifth food group, but just as quickly as it started, it went back into obscurity. Different types of hotels are (1) limited service, which means they don't have a coffee shop, restaurant, a bar, or room service; in other words, they don't have a full kitchen; (2) full-service hotels, which have room service, a restaurant, bar, large banquet rooms, laundry services, and other amenities; (3) extended-stay hotels, which are limited service and focus on guests looking to stay more than one night and typically five to seven days or more; (4) boutique hotels, which are usually high-end facilities with amenities like spas, normally do not have a major hotel flag such as Hilton or Holiday Inn, are usually owned by smaller companies, and are in markets where there are barriers to entry and the guests don't want to stay at a name-brand hotel. For instance, in downtown Santa Fe, there is only one large national chain hotel for one of the most visited cities in the United States. This is a property type for which there are a lot of conferences on lending, owning, and developing, as well as a number of monthly newsletters and similar periodicals that will help you get to know the players and work in this financing niche.

Apartments or multifamily properties: This is a niche in which many brokers have been extremely successful, mainly because almost all lenders like to make loans on apartments. They are considered one of the most stable property types to finance, except in overbuilt markets. This is also one of the most competitive property types. Apartments are classified as class A, B, C, and D. Some lenders will finance only class A luxury apartments; many lenders will finance B, C, and D properties. Apartment owners seem to be more in touch with direct financing than owners of other property types, except possibly hotels. So it is more difficult to focus on only the Class A properties because you will often find yourself competing with lenders calling on these owners. With class B and below, there is much less competition directly from lenders, and these buildings tend to fly under the radar of many brokers, so it is a great niche and can be extremely profitable if that becomes your focus.

Apartments also include senior housing and student housing. There are lenders that specialize in both. Student housing near a university will have much more scrutiny. The one thing to be aware of is whether the students are paying a market rent. In some areas where a single apartment unit may rent for $1,000 per month, two students each pay $700 to $1,000 per month. The lender would probably discount that rent to the market rent of $1,000 per month. Senior housing is typically very stable and looked upon favorably by most lenders that finance apartments.

Assisted living facilities: These types of properties generally have different levels of health care provided by the facility and are looked at based on the levels of care. One reason is that the higher the level of care, the more licensing is required and the more difficult it would be for a lender to manage the property in the event of a default. With that said, this is a great niche that will only get better as the population ages. Many lenders like this property type.

Credit tenant or investment-grade tenant properties: This is another well-liked property type for lenders because the better the financial strength of the tenant, the less risk of the loan having problems. These can be any type of property with a strong tenant. In fact, for a period several years ago, a borrower could borrow 100 percent of the value of the property with a loan term coterminous with the credit lease, and at the end of the term the borrower would own the property with no debt. These properties were considered similar to bonds because of the credit of the tenant. In those cases, the tenant had to be responsible for all repairs and maintenance of the property, what we call an absolute lease. Although fairly rare now, examples of today's credit tenant properties are Walgreen's, Costco, Federal Express, and Wal-Mart. They are more common as retail properties, but could be offices, such as Allstate Insurance (which I working on a deal for now), industrial warehouses like Coca Cola or Wal-Mart, or a restaurant like McDonald's or Chili's (if the parent company Brinker's Intl. is on the lease). This can be a good niche if you keep up with the lenders because you can win a lot of deals if you just know what is available. Lenders today vary a lot on how aggressive they will be on different credit leases. For instance, if you and your competition know a certain lender has financed a lot of Walgreen's properties, you may look for a different lender because the first lender, while just recently closing loans on them, may not want to increase their exposure, or

be what we call full on that credit. That is why it is important to keep up with what lenders are doing what loans on
credit tenant leases.

Industrial: This term can refer to big warehouses for storage,
big warehouses with manufacturing, or office/warehouse
property that is also referred to as flex space. One of the
first things that comes up with lenders for these properties
is the type of construction. Many lenders will not lend on
metal buildings. The other item that always comes up is
the use of the property by the tenant and the possibility
of any environmental contamination issues at the subject
or adjacent properties. With that said, most lenders really
like this property type, especially clean warehouse projects.
There are not enough to go around, so most lenders get
excited when you approach them with one—a great niche.

Mobile home parks and self-storage: I discuss these two
together because many lenders who like one like both property types. With mobile home parks, you want projects with
curbs and gutters, asphalt drives, and concrete pads for the
homes. They used to be rated by stars, with a five-star park
the best, but one of the requirements of the five-star park
was that it was not too old. Because very few new parks are
being constructed today, there are very few five-star parks.
Infill, well-matured, and senior parks are really sought after
by the lending community, as well as the snowbird parks
that are occupied only in the winter months, when seniors
leave their cold winter homes and head for these warmer
climates. With self-storage, lenders like nonmetal construction but will finance both. Stabilized properties with several
years of consistent income are preferred.

Convenience stores and gas stations: This is great niche
because it is very difficult to find many lenders to finance

them. The convenience store is as much a business as it is real estate, and all lenders are worried about environmental contamination with gas stations. I have seen a number of people finance entire portfolios of these at one time, which can be very lucrative and makes sense because they tend to have one operator with many units in a single market or a single state.

General Services Administration (GSA) properties: On the development side, many developers have done very well with properties that have the some form of the federal government as the tenant. They can be the Social Security Administration, U.S. Customs, Border Patrol, Homeland Security, Health and Human Services, and many others. There are normally two issues with these properties that prevent many lenders from having much interest. First, in many cases the government is paying is above market for the leases. Second, the leases very often have cancellation clauses or appropriations clauses, both of which allow them to walk from the lease. So if the tenant leaves, not only do you have to retenant the space; you have to retenant a space at an above-market rent, which is impossible. The argument in favor of these properties is that the government bureaucracy is so slow that they never terminate a lease prior to expiration and, in fact, are much more likely to exercise an option to extend the lease beyond the initial term.

Acquisition and development (A&D) residential and condominiums: Both were very popular during the last 5 to 10 years but are much more difficult to finance in today's world. That makes it a good niche, because you should get paid more for finding a more difficult loan.

Specialty lenders: This will make a great niche in the coming years. Rather than focus on a property type, focus on certain lending types, such as equity investors, bridge lenders, and hard-money lenders. Again, these may allow you to earn a large fee on a loan as well. Along the same lines, you can become a market expert, too. If you are in a large city like Los Angeles, you may want to focus on one area and always know everything going on in your market rather than driving all over the place and always having to start over in a new market.

Finally, look into many conferences and periodicals on the lender or property type you want to make your niche, and then start attending them and meeting the owners and lenders in your arena. To have a niche, you need to become an expert in that area and know everything there is to know, so that anyone looking for loans in that niche will have to come to you.

Index